INDONESIA

Number 109 April 2020

Published by Southeast Asia Program Publications • Cornell University Press

Contributing Editors: Joshua Barker, Eric Tagliacozzo

Editorial Advisory Board

Audrey Kahin	Claude Guillot	Hendrik Maier
Kaja McGowan	Danilyn Rutherford	Rudolf Mrázek

Submissions: Submit manuscript as double-spaced document in MS word or similar. Please format citation and footnotes according to the style guidelines in *The Chicago Manual of Style*, 16th edition.

Address: Please address all correspondence and manuscripts to the managing editor at sg265@cornell.edu. We prefer electronic submissions.

Reprints: Contributors will receive one complimentary copy of the issue in which their articles appear.

Abstracts: Abstracts of articles published in *Indonesia* appear in *Excerpta Indonesica*, which is published semiannually by the Royal Institute of Linguistics and Anthropology, Leiden. Articles appearing in this journal are also abstracted and indexed in *Historical Abstracts* and *America: History and Life*.

Subscription information: Contact journals@longleafservices.org for more information. Digital subscriptions for individuals and institutions are handled by JSTOR (participation@jstor.org) and Project Muse (muse@jhu.press.edu).

INDONESIA online: All *Indonesia* articles published at least five years prior to the date of the current issue are accessible to our readers on the internet free of charge. For more information concerning annual print and online subscriptions, pay-per-view access to recent articles, and access to our archives, please see: **seap.einaudi.cornell.edu/indonesia_journal** or https://ecommons.cornell.edu/handle/1813/52499

Cover: Mary Steedly's office door at the Department of Anthropology, Harvard University, December 2018. Photo by Carla Jones.

SEAP Publications Staff:
Managing Editor	Sarah E. M. Grossman
Assistant Editor	Fred L. Conner

ISBN-13: 978-1-5017-5477-7
ISSN 0019-7289
© 2020 Cornell University

Table of Contents 109

Special Issue
Mary Steedly's Anthropology of Modern Indonesia: A Collection of Keywords
Smita Lahiri, Patricia Spyer, and Karen Strassler, eds.

Introduction—Someone Else Speaking: Reflections on Mary Steedly as Author and Anthropologist, *Smita Lahiri, Patricia Spyer, and Karen Strassler*	1
Eating an Elephant: Culinary Nationalism and the Memory of the Senses *Mary Margaret Steedly*	17
Narrative, *James Peacock*	31
Telltale, *Patricia Spyer*	37
Gender, *Carla Jones*	45
Culture, *Smita Lahiri*	51
Audience, *Ann Marie Leshkowich*	57
Specificity, *Juno Salazar Parreñas*	65
Nationalism, *Veronika Kusumaryati*	71
Outskirts, *Jesse Hession Grayman*	77
Spirits, *Manduhai Buyandelger*	85
Haunting, *Byron J. Good and Mary-Jo DelVecchio Good*	91
Memory, *Karen Strassler*	99
After All, *Kenneth M. George*	105
Mary Margaret Steedly: Selected Publications, *The Editors*	113
Reviews:	
Jemma Purdy, Antje Missbach, and Dave McRae. *Indonesia: State & Society in Transition.* Boulder and London: Lynne Rienner, 2020. *Robert W. Hefner*	115

Nobutu Yamamoto. *Censorship in Colonial Indonesia, 1901–1942.* Leiden: Brill, 2019.   119
   John Ingleson

Tim Lindsey and Simon Butt. *Indonesian Law.* Oxford: Oxford University Press, 2018.   123
   Jeremy J. Kingsley

Susie Protschky. *Photographic Subjects: Monarchy and Visual Culture in Colonial Indonesia.* Manchester: Manchester University Press, 2019.   125
   Arnout van der Meer

Jan Mrázek. *Wayang & Its Doubles: Javanese Puppet Theatre, Television and the Internet.* Singapore: National University of Singapore Press, 2019.   129
   Miguel Escobar Varela

David Bourchier. *Illiberal Democracy in Indonesia: The Ideology of the Family State.* Abingdon: Routledge, 2015.   133
   Jeffrey A. Winters

Mary Steedly, summer 2017
(photo by Patricia Spyer)

Someone Else Speaking: Reflections on Mary Steedly as Author and Anthropologist

Smita Lahiri, Patricia Spyer, and Karen Strassler

When Mary Margaret Steedly died on a snowy morning in January 2018, modern Indonesian studies lost one of its most sensitive and incisive voices. As an anthropologist and oral historian, Mary's signal achievement was to delineate a series of overlooked figures located "on the outskirts" of the Indonesian nation, as well as to write their disruptive presence into authoritative accounts of nationalism, postcoloniality, history, violence, and state power, from which they had been excluded. A consummate practitioner of ethnography as both a form of investigation and as a genre of writing, Mary was keenly attuned to cultural poetics as well as to the textuality of her own writing. Instead of offering seamless counter-narratives or plainly intelligible voices, her body of work made room for—but refused to tame—a multitude of disjointed and indeterminate ways of inhabiting and imagining Indonesia, most notably from the perspectives of (mostly) non-elite, rural, and peri-urban Karo Batak women. Above all, Mary's exquisite ear for the ephemerality and density of stories—including what they left unsaid—registered the wit and personalities of people whose words were rarely accorded value within their own society, let alone by outsiders.

Smita Lahiri is a lecturer in anthropology and international affairs at the University of New Hampshire; Patricia Spyer is a professor of anthropology at the Graduate Institute, Geneva, Switzerland; and Karen Strassler is an associate professor in the department of anthropology at Queens College and the Graduate Center of City University of New York.

All three of us have the good fortune to count Mary as a mentor or collaborator, and our respective friendships with her were longstanding and particular. This issue of *Indonesia* realizes our initial vision of a collection of essays emphasizing her groundbreaking contributions to anthropology, feminist studies, and the study of Indonesia. In the process of compiling them, something additional has come to light. Nearly all of the pieces included here originated as oral presentations by Mary's colleagues and students at two memorial events, both of which we helped organize.[1] Not surprisingly, many of these brief expository essays include reminiscences of Mary by people who felt close to her. As they make clear, Mary's deep and generative commitment to interlocutors, students, and colleagues demands to be acknowledged in its own right. Taken as a whole, this multivocal tribute reflects and reaffirms a central conviction of Mary's entire body of work, namely, that "voices are never singular, meaning is always negotiated, and there is room in any story for someone else's speaking."[2]

Personal and Intellectual Background

The daughter of a faculty member at the Citadel, Mary grew up in Charleston, South Carolina, on the campus of the storied military college. Ever a southerner at heart, she became acquainted early on with the ghosts of pasts that would not stay put. Throughout her life, she remained acutely attuned to obliqueness, silences, and the whole range of means by which things that cannot or will not be spoken of nonetheless find their way into language.

Mary's path into academia was neither straight nor speedy: she graduated with an undergraduate degree in business administration, and did not earn her Ph.D. in anthropology until well after turning forty. Like many of the pioneering Boasian anthropologists whose writings she enjoyed and admired (particularly those with unconventional career trajectories that were shaped by constraints of race and gender), Mary reinvented herself and her circumstances with creativity and perseverance. After receiving a bachelor's degree from the University of North Carolina at Greensboro, she worked as a receptionist in the Folklore department at the University of North Carolina at Chapel Hill. This circumstance piqued her interest in studying people's lives and stories, leading her into the master's program in folklore, where she

---

[1] Two events honoring Mary Steedly were held during the last months of 2018. A round table entitled "The Said and the Unsaid: Honoring the Legacy of Mary Margaret Steedly" was convened at the American Anthropological Association meetings in San Jose, California, in late November 2018. Two weeks later a symposium entitled "Other Voices, Other Stories: Ethnographic Legacies of Mary Margaret Steedly" was held at Harvard University, bringing together many of Mary's former students for an extraordinary day of reflections on her role in their development as scholars. This collection includes the papers from the round table as well as three papers on Indonesia and Malaysia from the symposium. We also solicited contributions from Mary's longtime colleagues, Byron and Mary Jo DelVecchio Good, as well as an afterword from Kenneth George, her colleague and dear friend since graduate school. There were many who celebrated Mary's work with us but could not be included in this collection. At the Harvard symposium, moving and insightful tributes were presented by former students Lilith Mahmud, Akin Hubbard, Tahmima Anam, Tashi Rabgey, Namita Dharia, Jennifer Mack, Julia Yezbick, Stephanie Spray, and Diana Allen; and by colleagues Michael Herzfeld and Lucien Taylor. We would also like to mention Lindsay French, Maple Rasza, and Haley Duschinsky, who were prevented from participating by last-minute circumstances, and Doreen Lee, who helped envision the AAA roundtable.

[2] Mary Margaret Steedly, *Hanging without a Rope: Narrative Experience in Colonial and Postcolonial Karoland* (Princeton: Princeton University Press, 1993), 201.

discovered anthropology and Indonesia through James Peacock and the writings of Clifford Geertz. Mary's first major ethnographic project brought her into sustained contact with the storied Lumbee faith healer Vernon Cooper, leaving her with a deep respect for unofficial expertise and an abiding interest in the power of unseen things (see James Peacock's essay in this collection). She would later describe this work as formative in teaching her to yield to the incompleteness of any account, the limits of the ethnographer's own understanding, and the importance of paying clear-sighted attention to "the stories people *want* to tell, not just to the ones that we want them to tell us" (see Ken George's essay in this collection).[3]

Mary entered the field of anthropology at the height of its "reflexive turn," which highlighted the textual politics of ethnographic writing, threw open the gates to literary and historical influences, and activated a prolonged state of ferment in which feminist, Marxist, and postcolonial critiques played important roles. All of this left a deep imprint on Mary's thought and practice. While pursuing her doctorate at the University of Michigan under the guidance of Mick Taussig and Sherry Ortner, she continued to hone the legacies of her apprenticeship as a folklorist, most notably her sensitivity to how context and audience shape a story as it is told. And at a time when many anthropologists were retreating from the culture paradigm, Mary developed a lasting regard and affection for the more idiosyncratic figures of Boasian cultural anthropology, including Zora Neale Hurston, Margaret Mead, and Boas himself (see Smita Lahiri's essay in this collection).

Mary joined the Harvard faculty in 1990, a few years before the publication of her first book, the prize-winning *Hanging without a Rope*, which was based on her dissertation research in the hilly Karo-speaking region of West Sumatra. In 1998, she became the first woman to be promoted to tenure within the ranks of Harvard's anthropology department. There she remained until the end, commanding a level of respect and regard that would be difficult to overstate. Mary was one of those people (every department seems to have them) who do more than their share to keep things on track. She was an adept, if at times reluctant, administrator, for she vastly preferred mentoring and teaching. While she kept students and colleagues on their toes and periodically ran out of lost her patience with them, she was unflagging in her support of graduate students, particularly international students, as well as junior faculty and fellows like Smita Lahiri and Karen Strassler, whom she had a hand in recruiting. Behind Mary's unsentimental manner lay a deep kindness for and investment in her students. While she demanded an exacting level of context and specificity from their work (see Juno Parreñas's essay in this collection), she never sought to cast her students in her own mold, but instead encouraged them to discover and develop their own voices.

While Mary was deeply conscious of having landed at the most elite of institutions, she was neither fazed nor entranced by Harvard's grandeur. As one of the first members of the department to have been granted tenure from within, she knew that for all its perks and privileges, Harvard could be a chilly place for women, junior faculty, and anyone who did not fit in for one reason or another. Instead of

---

[3] Mary Margaret Steedly, "Author's Response: Mary Margaret Steedly," in "Reviewed Work(s): *Rifle Reports: A Story of Indonesian Independence*, by Mary Margaret Steedly," *Sojourn* 30, 3 (November 2015): 874.

succumbing to Harvard's hierarchical traditionalism or symbolic campaigns to buck it, she focused on making it a place where outsiders (in whom she saw herself) could find what they needed to thrive. Her web of relational commitments drew much of her time and energy, sometimes at the expense of the writing projects that were her true passion.

After *Hanging without a Rope*, Mary would go on to write numerous articles as well as her magnificent *Rifle Reports*, which was based on extensive archival and oral history research.[4] In collaboration with Patsy Spyer, with whom she enjoyed a decades-long friendship and intellectual bond, Mary co-edited the volume *Images That Move*, a reflection of her growing interest in images, visuality, media, and publics.[5] At the time of her death, she was writing a book on the military college where she spent her childhood.

We begin this discussion of her scholarship by turning to the unique ethnographic sensibility that led Mary to sail against the prevailing winds of the academy, informing her important interventions within scholarship about gender and power, colonial and postcolonial discourse, as well as history and memory. Subsequently, we follow a more-or-less chronological order as we reflect on Mary's foundational 1993 monograph, *Hanging without a Rope*, an innovative regional ethnography whose insights she would further develop in her 2013 masterpiece, *Rifle Reports*, an ethnographic history of the struggle for Indonesian independence during 1945–49 and how it was remembered afterwards. We also take note of the varied interests Mary cultivated in the intervening years between these two companion volumes. During this time, she incorporated such themes as place, media, and sensory experience into new explorations of Indonesian nation-making within the post-authoritarian public culture that emerged after the New Order unraveled in 1998.

Post-Reflexivity: Ethnography as Practice and as Genre

Like the quilts made by women in the American South that Mary coveted and collected, Mary's ethnographic practice was a meticulous craft marked by careful labor, imaginative virtuosity, and sheer pleasure in language and conversation. Mary was—as we all are—a product of her time, yet she assimilated the concerns and innovations of her discipline in an alchemy whose results were highly original and uniquely her own.

As we have noted, Mary's scholarly formation was strongly influenced by the move towards reflexivity that began in the mid-1980s, when anthropologists trained a new level of critical attention on their own textual creations and took stock of their positions as embodied observers. Yet in her own writing, Mary largely eschewed the self-preoccupation and marked experimentalism of the moment. She notably avoided "the paper I," her name for the dominant authorial presence that pervaded many paradigmatic examples of reflexive ethnography. Rather, the way Mary's authorial

---

[4] Mary Margaret Steedly, *Rifle Reports: A Story of Indonesian Independence* (Berkeley: University of California Press, 2013).

[5] Patricia Spyer and Mary Margaret Steedly, eds., *Images That Move* (Santa Fe: School for Advanced Research Press, 2013).

presence pervades her writing can best be understood in relation to an idea to which she insisted on calling attention, namely, the distinction between *ethnography as practice and as genre*. (The phrase became the title of one of her most popular courses, one which influenced several cohorts of Harvard anthropology students.)

The relationship between empiricism and textuality has intrigued many literary critics, among them that magisterial analyst of colonialism's textual politics, Edward Said. Mary particularly liked Said's essay, "Representing the Colonized," where he admits his unlikely affection for the very discipline that has often (and rightly) been called the "handmaiden" of colonialism.[6] The essay can be read as an effort to understand the peculiar effect of "deep down freshness" (a phrase Said took from the poet Gerald Manley Hopkins) retained by a select number of classic ethnographies long after they had become outdated.[7] Said concluded that the source of their power lay in a certain type of labor submerged (and often artfully concealed) in the text—namely, the slow, obsessive work of the anthropologist–author in remembering and giving a second life to the events and emotions he had witnessed and experienced fleetingly and *in situ*. The paradoxical freshness that struck Said so deeply can be felt on every page of *Hanging without a Rope* and *Rifle Reports*. In keeping with the spirit of her time, however, Mary achieved this artful effect by disclosing rather than concealing the broader circumstances and quotidian dynamics of her research.

One of Mary's main objections to the "paper I" was that it risked collapsing the gap between different orders of anthropological experience: the time and place of field research itself and the moment and milieu of writing about it. Mary was ever-alert to the mercurial quality of memory, ever-committed to a feminist view of knowledge as partial, positioned, and contextual. For her, reflexivity meant embracing the non-identity of the "I" who conducted interviews, wrote fieldnotes, and formed impressions with the "I" who imposed coherence upon it all at a temporal remove. To convey in one's writing both the messiness of fieldwork and the unruly fabrications of authorship was to acknowledge the reality that "any text is a patchwork of other peoples' words and ideas."[8] For Mary, this was at once an ethical and an artistic stance: a way of sticking to the facts (which, as noted earlier, included "attending to the stories people *want* to tell"), but also of marking the parameters of the creative and interpretive liberties she allowed herself.

Mary's engagement with the postcolonial can be discerned at many levels, including in the ways that she practiced without fanfare her commitment to a decolonized feminist anthropology. Newly reflexive about their craft and their own imbrication in structures of power, many anthropologists working in the 1990s gravitated toward research and writing projects that highlighted past and present resistance on the part of marginalized groups. As scholars began to hold themselves accountable to their interlocutors in new ways, as well as to proclaim solidarity with

---

[6] Edward W. Said, "Representing the Colonized: Anthropology's Interlocutors," *Critical Inquiry* 15, 2 (Winter 1989): 205–25. All of Said's examples were by men, so the masculine pronoun is used here advisedly.

[7] Said, "Representing the Colonized," 213.

[8] Steedly, *Hanging without a Rope*, 67. *Hanging without a Rope* was co-winner of the Society for Humanistic Anthropology's 1994 Victor Turner Prize for best ethnography. It was also co-winner of the Chicago Folklore Prize.

social and political struggles, they also encountered new predicaments of authorship. These were sharply delineated by Sherry Ortner, who diagnosed the rise of "ethnographic refusal" as a sign of something both commendable and worrying. Ortner acknowledged that practicing anthropology more responsibly might mean permitting one's informants' interests and projects to bear decisively upon one's own writing choices. At the same time, Ortner feared that doing so might result in ethnographies that had been redacted of precisely the kinds of nuances needed for the portrayal of people as full and complex political subjects.[9]

It is safe to say that Mary's work was the antithesis of refusal as characterized by Ortner. Instead of tidying up the messy heterogeneity of Karo accounts, Mary chose to hew close to their contours, leaving their gaps, incoherencies, and oddities unsmoothed. Mimetic of lived experience, her texts wove fragments of speech and action into narratives that never resolved into neat plots or simple messages, but hummed with unexpressed emotion and a plenitude of possible meanings.

Mary's circumspection when it came to relating the lives of others also came close in spirit to the positive forms of "refusal" that are being rearticulated by a new generation of scholars. Offering a closer appreciation of withholding as practiced by themselves as well as their interlocutors, the refusal in this newer wave signifies varied forms of relational work that can defend and generate valued forms of sociality.[10] In a related vein, Mary declined to presume that she could access interior, subjective experience, instead carefully circumscribing her exercise of ethnographic authority to what she learned from shared stories and conversation. To do ethnography was first and foremost to position oneself as a *listener* (see Ann Marie Leshkowich's essay in this collection). By her own account, Mary steered clear of certain forms and conventions—the life history, for example—out of reluctance to turn singular individuals into personifications of historical or social forces. And at a time when anthropologists were increasingly making their names with mannered and abstract forms of theorizing, she also pointedly eschewed any kind of posturing and heavy-handedness.

The relationship between theory and data in Mary's ethnographic writing might be likened to those forms of embroidery in which the most intricate needlework remains out of sight on the underside of the fabric, enhancing the play of light and shadow on the side that faces outward. She found inspiration in a wide range of places within and beyond anthropology and Southeast Asian studies, including fiction, literary and film criticism, Marxist and post-Marxist aesthetics, cultural studies, critical theory, feminist historiography and media studies. Faulkner, Calvino, Bakhtin, Benjamin, and Barthes were just a few of her touchstones, all of whom attended to "the dense, heterogeneous entangling of lives, stories, and desires."[11] But while Mary could easily have centered her writing around engagements with any number of theorists, she chose instead to subordinate theorizing to story, event, and context. Her critical and theoretical infrastructure did little to distract from the ethnographic life-world: the particular people with whom she spoke, their fragmentary and evocative narratives, and the

---

[9] Sherry B. Ortner, "Resistance and the Problem of Ethnographic Refusal," *Comparative Study of Society and History* 7, 1 (1995): 173–93.

[10] See, for example, Carole McGranahan, "Theorizing Refusal: An Introduction," *Cultural Anthropology* 31, 3 (2016): 319–25.

[11] Steedly, *Hanging without a Rope,* 22.

storied landscapes they inhabited. She embedded her analysis and interpretation within the material itself,[12] showing rather than telling the complexities of person, place, and predicament.

To put this a little differently: in the freshness of Mary's writing, we can feel her desire to let the material breathe, to let things remain a little "obtuse."[13] Writing was especially laborious for Mary because she challenged herself to create a subtle underpinning of structure without rendering her account too neat and linear. How to render illegibility just legible enough without stripping its opaque qualities, how to show the power of repetition without being redundant, how to make gaps and silences speak? It took deliberate, painstaking artistry to retain a hint of strangeness within the canvas of a prose style that was lucid, measured, and precise.

Here, surely, lies another variety of "refusal." Mary wrote to please herself and at her own pace, caring little about being a "productive" scholar. While the academy heaped rewards on the speedy and the prolific, she worked slowly and patiently, letting her ideas mature and crafting her texts with meticulous care. Confident that her work demanded—and deserved—time to come to fruition, she never settled into complacency when it came to her writing. She once remarked that each time she finished a difficult piece of writing, she hoped that at last she'd figured out her formula—only to find that the next project demanded a method of its own.

Ethnographic History: An Anthropologist amongst the Nationalists

Hanging without a Rope rendered the nation from the oblique angle of its geographic and social "borderlands."[14] This move was not merely a matter of supplementing existing studies, for it effected a fundamental unsettling of dominant frameworks and narratives, both those produced by scholars and those that circulated within Indonesia as official and popular accounts of national history. The healers, market traders, spirits, and others whose stories she told were (mostly) women for whom the "central interpretive devices" of the nation—those of "development," "tradition," and "modernity"—didn't "quite work."[15] Reading Karo accounts against colonial texts, Mary demonstrated that Karo postcolonial experiences of being "out of step" were rooted in colonial efforts to impose Christianity, to squeeze Karo animist practices into a narrowly defined realm of *adat* (custom), and to install a rationalized market economy. Against a presumption of rupture between the colonial and postcolonial, Mary showed how these impositions continued into the postcolonial period, finding

---

[12] See Smita Lahiri, "On Nonrecognition and Feminist Epistemology: Doing Ethnographic Theory with Mary Steedly," *Network of Ethnographic Theory*, January 2019, https://networkofethnographictheory.wordpress.com/on-nonrecognition-and-feminist-epistemology-doing-ethnographic-theory-with-mary-steedly/

[13] On "the obtuse," see: Steedly, *Hanging without a Rope*, 136–37; and Roland Barthes, "The Third Meaning: Critical Essays on Music, Art, and Representation," in Roland Barthes," *The Responsibility of Forms*, trans. R. Howard (New York: Farrar, Straus and Giroux, 1985), 41–62.

[14] In exploring the Indonesian "outskirts," Mary was joined by a cohort of scholars, including Patricia Spyer, Webb Keane, Anna Tsing, Janet Hoskins, Ken George, and Danilyn Rutherford (among many others).

[15] Carolyn Kay Steedman, *Landscape for a Good Woman: A Story of Two Lives* (New Brunswick: Rutgers University Press, 1987), 5.

Mount Sibayak, Karoland, Indonesia, 1994 (photo by Karen Strassler)

especially powerful reinforcement in New Order projects of development and discipline. From the vantage point of the Karo highlands, the state—both colonial and postcolonial—made its presence felt less through the direct exertion of force than through the ability to promote powerful interpretations that excluded and proscribed others, leaving people "hanging without a rope." But while Mary did not celebrate "resistance," she also showed that "on the borderland of official order," state power was always limited; state projects and national ideologies were always subject to misrecognition, evasion, and alteration by those they intended to transform and control.[16]

Mary's second book, *Rifle Reports: A Story of Indonesian Independence*, further developed themes she had worked through in *Hanging without a Rope*, within the more ambitious scope of "ethnographic history." Conjuring the Indonesian revolution from the vantage point of the North Sumatran highlands, *Rifle Reports* pointedly took on the highly visible, discursively overworked, and ideologically saturated topics of revolution, nationalism, and national history. In *Rifle Reports*, we see both continuity with long-standing preoccupations as well as new dimensions of her thought and craft: a heightened concern with the visual and the sensory, an investigation of the scaled production of national time and space, and an effort to recuperate the open-ended, utopian quality of the nation *in medias res*, when nobody knew how things would turn out.

---

[16] Steedly, *Hanging without a Rope*, 118. See also her critique of overly monolithic accounts of state power: "To think of states as 'weak' or fragmented is not to deny the pervasiveness of power, but rather to understand it as dispersed and polyvalent rather than emanating from exemplary centers in Jakarta, Hanoi, or Bangkok" (Mary Margaret Steedly, "The State of Culture Theory in the Anthropology of Southeast Asia," *Annual Review of Anthropology* 28 [1999]: 444).

With *Rifle Reports,* Mary entered a field of Indonesian studies in which a focus on Java and a presumption of masculine agency predominated (see Veronika Kusumaryati's essay in this collection). Mary's account of the Independence struggle powerfully undercut a mythic "national narrative of disciplined military action and individual bravery, focused on a series of heroic (male) figures and iconic (Javanese) battles."[17] In drawing attention to the memories of Karo women, Mary effected a shift in the narrativization of national beginnings from one highlighting political parties, mass organizations, international diplomacy, and military actions, to one grounded in the aspirations and efforts of ordinary people who witnessed and joined in the project of nation in a location remote from the centers of power. Here, ideological commitments and nationalist rhetoric came through in half-understood fragments and talismanic words. Seismic historical events were deeply felt, but tended to be filtered in and through the overriding demands of everyday survival, a task that mostly fell to women. Even when writing about periods of extreme violence, Mary drew attention less to spectacular scenes of brutality than to the more quotidian and durable effects of violent events on ordinary familial and communal life in the form of unquiet spirits, fragmented memories, and painful silences (see Jesse Grayman's essay in this collection).

Mary's concern with gender yielded a focus on women that was never exclusive. As Benedict Anderson would eventually observe in his admiring review of *Rifle Reports,* "the signal beauty of Mary's work is that she writes about all kinds of Karo women, whether individuals or groups—without neglecting the Karo males."[18] It was above all Mary's sensitivity to how power worked to silence or dampen the voices of some and to amplify others, to render some accounts durable and others ephemeral, that marked her feminist approach to ethnography.

Yet even as it challenged the masculinist cast and heroic plotlines of nationalist history, Mary's account also acknowledged—and illuminated anew—the enduring potency of dreams of nationhood, freedom, and modernity, for women as well as for men. Women, Mary showed, were not merely victims, passive onlookers, or exceptional warriors in a male mold—the roles typically laid out for them in accounts of nationalist history—but enthusiastic participants in the project of nationhood who seized opportunities to imagine and forge new gendered forms of agency (see Carla Jones's essay in this collection). For the "eager" (*liar,* or wild, unruly) women she wrote about, *merdeka* (freedom) promised possibilities for independence of various kinds: for travel, education, choice in marriage, and so on.

Rifle Reports remarkably achieves an account of the past in a subjunctive mood, an account, in other words, that retains a sense of "how it felt to be alive to a moment in which there were no certain endings."[19] Praising the book as "path breaking," Anderson observed that Mary highlighted the unruly energies of an unfinished and unachieved social revolution that accompanied the anticolonial struggle for nationhood. The radical potentials of *revolusi* (revolution) would later be narratively and politically domesticated, cleansed of internal violence, chaos, and uncertainty,

---

[17] Steedly, "Author's Response: Mary Margaret Steedly," 870.
[18] Benedict R. O'G. Anderson, "Review Essay 1," in "Reviewed Work(s): *Rifle Reports,*" 862.
[19] This is the final line of the book; see Steedly, *Rifle Reports,* 324.

within an account of the "'War of Independence' in which only the military were proclaimed as national heroes."[20] Mary showed that the Independence struggle was more than a series of events with a predetermined ending; things might have turned out otherwise. The revolution, above all, was an emergent experience—and experience, for Mary, always comprised not only what actually happened but also what people told about what happened, what they were unable to say, as well as what they imagined might happen in the future. As Lesley Dwyer wrote in her review of *Rifle Reports*, Mary was highly attuned to "the danger of being seduced into a foreclosed facticity that fails to account for multiple storylines, some of which fail to circulate socially."[21] Writing forensically, as Mary put it, meant confronting such complexity, rather than dissolving it. It meant retaining a sense of puzzlement rather than solving the puzzle.

Even as she conveyed the past in all its open-ended multiplicity, Mary also foregrounded the present-day stakes of people's telling, attending to how people's memories of participation in the revolution could authorize moral claims to belonging in the nation. Mary based *Rifle Reports* upon diverse primary sources and interviews with elderly men and women who recalled upheavals in Karoland during 1945–49 from the vantage point of the 1990s. Despite its seemingly tight focus on the revolutionary era, the book discloses the inscription of experience in official history, personal memory, and the senses—at the time as well as afterward. The book thus illuminates how Karo men and women gradually became "Indonesians," too. What was transformative was not just the experience of the revolution itself. Subsequent patterns of practice and habit—of repeatedly honoring and parlaying certain kinds of experiences and of regarding others as too slight or terrifying to revisit—were equally constitutive.

This sensitivity to memories as a "political idiom" and as "a moving force in the lived-in present" is a defining characteristic of what Mary called "ethnographic history" and distinguishes it from historical anthropology,[22] oral history, ethnohistory and other related approaches:

> Ethnographic history embeds narrative experience in a complex temporal field which is not simply the "then" of the story and the "now" of the telling. It recognizes all the cumulative reworkings that narrative experience has undergone in between, through the array of audiences to which it has been presented and the broader storied field that it has occupied and may occupy in the future."[23]

Mary thus resisted the scholarly desire to excavate reliable "facts" about the past, but she also rejected analyses that would reduce memories to present-day constructions; instead, she challenged us to recognize what Trouillot called "the power in the story."[24]

---

[20] Anderson, "Review Essay 1," 861.
[21] Leslie Dwyer, "Review Essay 2," in "Reviewed Work(s): *Rifle Reports*," 864.
[22] Renato Rosaldo, *Ilongot Headhunting, 1883–1974* (Stanford: Stanford University Press, 1980), 31.
[23] Steedly, "Author's Response: Mary Margaret Steedly," 870–71.
[24] Michel-Rolph Trouillot, *Silencing the Past: Power and the Production of History* (Boston: Beacon Press, 1995).

As richly embedded as they are in the particularities of local places, *Hanging without a Rope* and *Rifle Reports* also intervene in the study of Indonesian history and nation through their suggestive reworking of the familiar opposition between "center" and "margin." Perhaps the sense of ambivalence and of only partial incorporation she identified among the Karo Batak of the North Sumatran highlands was not just a condition of being on the "outskirts" in relation to a presumed center. Perhaps she gave us better insight into how people everywhere—even at the putative center— inhabit the broader political communities and temporalities within which they live their lives: through the prism of local concerns and struggles, through the burdens of everyday life, through anticipations of unrealized futures, through layered tellings of the past and what might have been, through experiences of being both interpellated and misrecognized. Indeed, even as she shifted her attention from the highly localized world of the Karo Batak to a post-authoritarian, mass-mediated "occult public sphere" with its urban, middle-class audiences, she drew attention to disruptive forms of spectrality that saturated the "center" with the uncanny force of the unseen. Perhaps, Mary's work provocatively suggests, "outskirts" of various kinds dwell within the center, too.

Emplaced, Sensory, Spectral: Politics and Poetics of the Everyday

These distinctive contributions to scholarship on Indonesian nation and nationalism emerged not only from Mary's focus on women's narratives but from her analytic explorations of place, the everyday, the sensorial, and the spectral. Mary's work offers a sustained account of the social production of the nation in everyday life. In this sense, *Hanging without a Rope* and *Rifle Reports* continue a line that runs from Anderson's seminal idea of the nation as an "imagined community" through Charles Taylor's subsequently elaborations of "modern social imaginaries" and Michael Warner's notion of "publics."[25] While these scholars focused on the dissemination of national imaginings through exemplary sites or texts, whether novels or newspapers, maps, theme parks, or museums, Mary did so by examining everyday narratives, including those concerned with experiences of place. Indonesia, of course, is a "place," but one beyond the scale of human experience. To apprehend Indonesia (or any other nation-state) *through* place is necessarily to engage with the extrapolative "work of the imagination"[26] carried out by citizen subjects, who learn to experience national space within the concreteness of the local, especially during extraordinary and memorable times.

The "natural magic of landscape" was a theme that Mary first explored in *Hanging without a Rope* in relation to such objects as "place names, paths, signs of habitation; the sense of space as formerly known or occupied, an awareness (perhaps illusory) of the pulses of life and event that once animated it, of narrative trails and thickets that intersect and become entangled."[27] Later, in *Rifle Reports*, she would show the

---

[25] See: Benedict Anderson, *Imagined Communities: Reflections on the Origin and Spread of Nationalism* (London: Verso, 1991 [second edition]); Charles Taylor, *Modern Social Imaginaries* (Durham: Duke University Press, 2003); and Michael Warner, *Publics and Counterpublics* (New York: Zone Books, 2005).

[26] Arjun Appadurai, "Disjuncture and Difference in the Global Cultural Economy," *Public Culture* 2, 2: 1–24.

[27] Steedly, *Hanging without a Rope*, 144, 147.

generative role of place and narrative in people's claim to national belonging. Karo women, as Mary shows, came to apprehend their new nation through dislocation and movement through unfamiliar landscapes. They do not say this (or anything like it) in their stories. Instead, their memories emphasize the stopping points and sojourns along their travels as well as the challenges of staying fed and clothed, the necessity of trusting strangers, the tears for those left behind, and the shock of sudden violence. Such narratives trace an "obtuse" angle of distance from everyday nationalism's common sense frameworks, yet in their own way do as much to laminate the nation upon local experience, literally under one's feet.[28] Perhaps the most persuasive evidence of this is the exceptional example Mary presents of the "memory artist," a virtuoso poet and performer who gained fame for composing and recording a *tour de force* to Karo tradition: a song cycle of the evacuation based on her own typically gendered evacuation experience (see Karen Strassler's essay in this collection).

Throughout Mary's career, the "everyday" remained an ongoing concern, figuring as an emergent and layered experiential terrain mediated by the thickets of tellings and retellings and inflected by gender, privilege, subject position, and locality. The everyday was shot through with the unfinished business of colonial departures and violence, by gendered structures of kinship and sociality, and by the sensuous materiality of daily living. Characteristically, she approached the everyday obliquely, from the edge of everyday experience—foregrounding the vantage of "someone else speaking," the expectations regarding the textures and familiarity of place upended by war, or the opportunities for "eager girls" that surfaced during *revolusi*'s unsettled times.

Although the everyday that most held Mary's attention was unpredictable, she never lost sight of how the inherent banality of daily life persists even under the most extraordinary of circumstances. In her hands the everyday never risked becoming an uncritical formulation or a backdrop to the noteworthy or spectacular. In Mary's 1999 *Annual Review* article, published a year after the New Order's tumultuous downfall, she reminds her readers to localize violence and to pay heed to "the landscape of the banal," to not forget "the things that don't fall apart … the ordinary routines of everyday life … when expectations hold."[29]

Mary took pleasure in the sensuous materiality of sociality and social life and wove it through her ethnography. Taste, smell, sound, touch, things seen, unseen, or half-seen—and even then uncertainly—contour the scenes of revolutionary fervor, longings for tractors and glass windows, the "delicious" sound of the new word *merdeka* moving across the Karo highlands, the deprivations captured in the memory of a bland meal. As she progressed in her work on the Indonesian *horror* film and television serial genre populated by ghosts, haunted modern buildings, and vengeful female spirits, collaborated with Patsy on the project that concluded with *Images That Move,* and co-taught an ethnographic film course with Lucien Castaing-Taylor (director of Harvard's Sensory Ethnography Lab), Mary's writing became more explicitly engaged with the visual, perceptual dimensions of everyday life, always conceived within a larger matrix of sensory experience.

---

[28] Steedly, *Hanging without a Rope*, 136–37.
[29] Steedly, "The State of Culture Theory."

Two examples will suffice, both from *Rifle Reports*. The first is the description with which Mary opens Chapter 3, "Imagining Independence," as she imagines how the news of Indonesia's independence reached the Karo highlands:

> As I picture this scene, the car full of young men and guns charges along the steep and twisting road leading down from the highlands with the noisy, reckless bravado of today's daredevil motorcyclists and fare-hungry bus drivers. Farmers stand in puzzled surprise as cries of Merdeka! Merdeka! drift across the fields where they are working. Idle men in roadside cafés are startled from their chess and coffee as the convertible roars past and then vanishes around another curve.[30]

Ever reflexive and meticulous, Mary pulls back from this compelling image to remind the reader that, while immensely seductive, imagination of the past is never very reliable and how her own, in this passage and others, "is probably too cinematic in its envisioning of life in wartime."[31] The second example is Mary's close scrutiny of a photograph she captioned "Youth style, 1940s" depicting five youthful male "freedom fighters."[32] Attending both to how such "photographs—most of them, of course, posed—come closest to a direct expression of youth style" and to the romantic nostalgia that feeds on such images, her analysis of how they contribute to "the romance of the struggle" is exemplary of the best scholarship on visual artifacts and questions of visuality.[33]

As tactile and sensorial as it was, Mary's rendering of the everyday always made room for the unseen. It is no coincidence that her last published work explored the boom in supernatural films and television in the post-Suharto period, a kind of looping back to concerns of her first book but in a mass-mediated, post-authoritarian modality. The move from the intensely local, place-based spirits of *Hanging without a Rope* to the unrooted apparitions that populated the early twentieth-century mediascape marked broad transformations in the mediated nature of experience in Indonesia, but the through line was the generative power of disruptive (and sometimes healing) forces that refused full legibility or ideological assimilation. Mary was preoccupied by spirits in part, to be sure, because they mattered greatly to her interlocutors—whether Karo villagers or urban film buffs—and she refused to simply explain them away as an epiphenomenon of some other cause. Spirits were simply part of the landscape of the everyday, participants in that thickly layered "narrative experience" she sought to convey. Mary did not conceptually distinguish the presence of spirits from the broader condition of "interhabitational ambiguity" in which we are always possessed by other agencies (see Manduhai Buyandelger's essay in this collection). Spirits also figured prominently in Mary's work as part of her broad understanding of the past as an untamed and always partially unassimilated force in the present. For Mary, experience was itself haunted: social life is shot through with pasts that refuse to go away, with

---

[30] Steedly, *Rifle Reports*, 113.
[31] Steedly, *Rifle Reports*, 114.
[32] Steedly, *Rifle Reports*, 129.
[33] Steedly, *Rifle Reports*, 113.

ghosts that keep exerting pressure and making claims as they inhabit places, bodies, and words (see Byron Good and Mary Jo DelVecchio Good's essay in this collection).

From "Eating an Elephant" to a Collection of Keywords

Occasionally in her writings we get a glimpse of Mary at work—discovering a box of bootleg cassettes in the dusty corner of a radio shop, catching her research assistants in a moment of hilarity in an improvised "project room," consulting Karo friends and informants about unfamiliar words and phrases while translating a *katoneng-katoneng* song, or reading Faulkner and feeling the warmth of the US South on a cold winter night in Cambridge, Massachusetts. By and large, she relied more on recordings of interviews than on field notes, although Patsy recalls being shown notebooks with batik covers, their pages pasted with dried leaves, Karo names scribbled alongside, when she visited Mary in Medan's Padang Bulan neighborhood in 1984.

We begin this collection with a previously unpublished paper by Mary, where we see her once more in the middle of things. "Eating an Elephant" offers insight into Mary's ethnographic praxis as an observer, listener, and writer, making it the perfect prelude to the keyword essays that constitute this multi-voiced appreciation of Mary Steedly by her colleagues and students. "Eating an Elephant" demonstrates Mary's extraordinary ability to draw rich insights from apparently insignificant, yet "telltale," details (see Patsy's essay in this collection). The essay showcases Mary's skill as a crafter of narratives, both distinctively authored and characteristically replete with other people's voices. In its reference to Orwell's autobiographical short story "Shooting an Elephant," it reflects Mary's openness to literature as a source of insight and inspiration. Finally, it displays her sense of humor and her refusal to elevate the story of the nation from its grounding in mud, hunger, death, confusion, and absurdity.

For the contributors to this collection, Mary's work has been formative and inspirational in a wide range of ways. The idea for a collection of "keyword" essays focusing on Mary's work emerged from our desire to elaborate this extraordinary legacy. At first glance, the decision to comb out and delineate a set of themes from Mary's layered prose might seem to be at odds with her own efforts to "sink" readers "ever deeper into the dense narrativity of everyday life."[34] We take the license of doing so advisedly, and for the sake of giving her luminous scholarship its due. The keywords featured in these essays were self-selected by their authors, so readers may find a certain amount of overlap as well as possible omissions as well. We have tried to represent Mary's multifaceted interests and the range of ways she inspired us, but we make no claim to comprehensiveness.

Much like the "eager girls," the young revolutionary women she wrote of in *Rifle Reports* (some of whose lives were also cut cruelly short), Mary was fully alive to the pleasures and surprises of experience. We offer this collection of essays as a remembrance of that "eager girl." May it inspire many more encounters with the

---

[34] Steedly, *Rifle Reports*, 69.

extraordinary work of Mary Margaret Steedly, enticing a fresh stream of readers into its strange and beautiful thickets.[35]

Mary Steedly's office door at the Department of Anthropology, Harvard University, December 2018 (photo by Karen Strassler)

---

[35] On narrative "thickets," see Steedly, *Rifle Reports*, 15, 169.

Eating an Elephant: Culinary Nationalism and the Memory of the Senses

Mary Margaret Steedly

This presentation is drawn in part, but with a slightly different spin, from my book *Rifle Reports: A Story of Indonesian Independence*.[1] The book is about nationalism and the Indonesian struggle for independence from Dutch colonial rule between 1945 and 1950, as these appeared from the perspective of a peasant community "on the outskirts of the nation." The project took me back to a place where I'd lived for three years, a decade earlier: the province of North Sumatra, specifically its lowland capital city, Medan, and the nearby upland district of Tanah Karo (Karoland). This was the setting

---

Mary Margaret Steedly (1946–2018) was born in Ann Arbor, Michigan, and raised in Charleston, South Carolina. She studied at the University of North Carolina–Greensboro, and earned an MA in folklore at the University of North Carolina–Chapel Hill. She later attended the University of Michigan, where she submitted a prize-winning thesis for her PhD in cultural and medical anthropology. Mary taught in Harvard's anthropology department since 1990, and became a full professor of anthropology there in 1998.

[1] Mary Margaret Steedly, *Rifle Reports: A Story of Indonesian Independence* (Berkeley: University of California Press, 2013). Mary presented this paper in March 2014 at Boston University. She presented an earlier version at a workshop at Harvard University in April 2012, where a number of people were invited to comment on draft chapters of Mary's monograph *Rifle Reports*. The minimal editing done here by Patsy Spyer aims to preserve Mary's distinctive voice, and the paper remains much as she presented it in 2014. Although Mary was clear that she did not want any excerpts from her subsequent, unfinished book project on the Citadel to be published, we, the contributing editors to this collection of essays, feel confident that she would not have objected to including this piece in our tribute to her. Presented for the last time in 2014, a year after the publication of *Rifle Reports*, the paper builds on this prior work that provides the wider context in which it may be read even without the benefit of additional commentary on her part. For these reasons, we felt it would be more than appropriate to have her voice represented in this way alongside our own.

of my first book, *Hanging without a Rope*, in which I explored the possibility of constructing a local history refracted through stories of encounters with spirits.[2]

In my earlier sojourn in Karoland, I was fascinated by the vivid stories of life during wartime that punctuated the everyday conversations of older Karo women and men I knew. These were told virtually at the drop of a hat—to my research team and to each other, to strangers on long-distance bus trips and over tea and cigarettes in streetside cafés, to their kids, neighbors and kin, in veterans groups, church meetings, and other public gatherings. But there was little recognition at the national level of their part in the Independence struggle, and few of the educated younger generation of Karo showed much knowledge of or interest in their stories. With the fiftieth anniversary of Independence taking place in 1995, it seemed important to record their accounts, especially those of women, whose contributions to the Independence struggle remained almost wholly unrecognized.

Between 1993 and 1995 my research assistants and I interviewed around 120 people about their experiences during the Independence struggle. They included former soldiers, militia officers, and government officials, as well as teachers, church elders, choir directors, midwives, nurses, entertainers, businesswomen, spirit mediums, and housewives, but the majority were small-scale farmers and traders. About three-quarters of them were women.

Some were people I had known for more than a decade; with others I had only the most transient of contacts. All but a few were ethnically self-identified as Karo. Many now lived in or around Medan, the sprawling capital of North Sumatra province, with their children or grandchildren, some had moved to Jakarta, but most remained in the towns and villages of the Karo highlands. Most were from the so-called Generation of '45, who came of age during the Independence struggle, and so their stories were no doubt colored by memories of youth, just as their experiences of the period were tinted by the enthusiasms and hopes of that adventurous life-phase. I collected local histories, self-published memoirs, photos from family albums, mimeographed testimonies and historical accounts, old recordings of songs, patriotic comic books, and much more. I read faded typescripts and listened to family stories, hoary jokes, and second- and third-hand yarns swapped in casual conversations in coffee shops and on bus trips. I haunted record shops and used-book stalls, attended Independence Day celebrations in the Karo highlands, explored archives in the Netherlands and in Jakarta, and was fortunate to receive from friends and colleagues copies of documents I never would have discovered on my own. Putting these materials together has been a long and laborious process, during which I have been grateful for the help and patience—as well as the impatience—of many friends and colleagues.

Indonesian national independence was declared on August 17, 1945, just days after the Japanese surrender that ended the Pacific War. Exactly five years later, on August 17, 1950, the Republic of Indonesia achieved full international recognition of its political sovereignty. Between these dates, Indonesians fought against Dutch efforts to retake their former archipelagic colony after three brutal years of Japanese occupation. Most Indonesians today refer to this period as the "struggle for independence" (I.,

---

[2] Mary Margaret Steedly, *Hanging without a Rope: Narrative Experience in Colonial and Postcolonial Karoland* (Princeton: Princeton University Press, 1993), 227.

perjuangan kemerdekaan). It was a time of military mobilization and political indoctrination, sporadic battles, diplomatic negotiations, and low-intensity guerrilla warfare. It was also a time of social turbulence, euphoric aspiration, and internal violence, during which Indonesians struggled not just to defeat the Dutch but also to move into a future that for many was barely imaginable.

This was the first successful war of anticolonial liberation in post-World War II Asia. Because of its historical precedence and predominantly nationalist (rather than Marxist-internationalist) orientation, as well as its success in welding a nation from diverse and dispersed populations—some thirteen thousand islands, several hundred linguistically and culturally differentiated groups—in a relatively short time *and* in the absence of some precolonial entity on which to base its territorial claims, Indonesia became a model and inspiration for theories of nationalism and state formation as well, from Clifford Geertz's work on new states in the 1960s to Benedict Anderson's on imagined communities in the 1980s.[3] During this time there has been a proliferation of local histories, memoirs, and biographies written by and about veterans and political leaders of the struggle. Nevertheless, most academic studies of the struggle, both in Indonesia and elsewhere, have continued to attend to a small segment of the total national spectrum, focusing geographically on Java, the nation's demographic and cultural center; politically on urban elites; and experientially on men. Without denying the centrality, both before and after the fact, of Java-based elite men in the project of postcolonial state formation, *Rifle Reports* shifts attention to one of the neglected parts of that spectrum: rural women and men in the Karo highlands of northern Sumatra.

Inspired by a political rhetoric that equated independence with such tokens of modernity as electric lights, tractors, and glass windows, Karo villagers embraced the nationalist cause with an enthusiasm perhaps unexpected in once-stateless hill people who had long been, in James Scott's phrase, adept at the "art of not being governed."[4] "With us," explained Eben Hezer Sinuraya, a former company commander in the largest of the Karo popular militias,

> ... as soon as the gong of Independence sounded, it was "forward march" right away! We didn't know what had to be done, but we stepped right up ... We stepped forward, even if we didn't know anything, we stepped forward. Later, from the inside, then we could fill it in. Otherwise, what is "Independence"? What is independence? At the time probably 80 percent of the Indonesian people didn't understand what independence meant, in political terms, they didn't understand. How could they understand independence, they didn't even know how to write! ... But as soon as there was the proclamation, they joined right in. Whether it was because they were afraid or whatever, well, that's

---

[3] Clifford Geertz, *The Interpretation of Cultures* (New York: Basic Books, 1973), Chapters 9, 10, 12, respectively, "After the Revolution: The Fate of Nationalism in the New States," "The Integrative Revolution: Primordial Sentiments and Civil Politics in the New States," and "Politics Past, Politics Present: Some Notes on the Uses of Anthropology in Understanding the New States"; and Benedict Anderson, *Imagined Communities: Reflections on the Origin and Spread of Nationalism*, revised edition (London: Verso, 1991).

[4] From James C. Scott, *The Art of Not Being Governed: An Anarchist History of Upland Southeast Asia* (New Haven: Yale University Press, 2010).

possible too, but it wasn't 100 percent because they were afraid. They really wanted to take part.[5]

Their enthusiasm flourished despite the privation and terror that ensued, as Karoland became a battleground and a "sea of fire" as Dutch troops gradually gained control of the district. Yet the reason for this enthusiasm is unclear, even to Karo themselves, as Eben Hezer's ambivalent statement suggests. Karo highlanders, who were touched lightly by the Dutch presence, would appear to have had little reason to oppose the reinstatement of colonial rule and little material with which to imagine the grand sweep of an archipelagic national community. Few were literate, and most had never traveled beyond the confines of their district. It may well be that they "really wanted to take part," as Eben Hezer said—but what did they think they were taking part in? What kind of collective identity might Karo have envisioned for themselves at the beginning of independence? For the most part, they had little sense either of "Indonesia" as a real or imagined entity, or even of "Karo" as an exclusive, perduring ethnic appellation. Freedom, as they imagined it, was "delicious"; it was the antithesis of "feeling colonized"; it was the opportunity to reopen old wounds, to redress old wrongs; it was a chance to step into a bright new future exemplified by glass windows, airplanes, tractors, and transistor radios.

Anthony Reid has recently characterized Indonesian nationalism as "anti-imperial," and argued that it was through the "alchemy of revolution" that an ascribed colonial identity (D., *inlander*, "native") was transformed into a "passionately felt new community." The anti-imperial struggles of Southeast Asian decolonization—in the Philippines, Vietnam, Burma, Indonesia—"sacralized the new identities which had been charted on the map by the old empires." Especially among the "state-averse" societies of the Southeast Asian uplands and elsewhere on the outskirts of state power, the colonial state was seen as an "essentially alien but necessary construct, which opened doors to a broader modernity than would otherwise be possible."[6] The Indonesian state took up the mantles of modernity and necessity that had been promised—but not delivered—by its colonial predecessors, both Dutch and Japanese, and attached them to a collective sense of national belonging.

Reid's assessment is a good descriptive summary of events and outcomes during the Indonesian independence struggle, but it is less satisfying as an explanation of anti-imperial nationalisms in places like Karoland. Nationalist commitment was, for one thing, not evenly spread across the archipelago, or even across the many ethnolinguistic communities of northern Sumatra. Why did Karo respond to the call for national independence, when other groups, most notably the Javanese plantation laborers who were unquestionably the most exploited population in the region, did not? Why did they take a more radical stance than their more cosmopolitan, better-educated Toba Batak neighbors? What significance could national belonging have had for people whose relations with neighboring groups had as often been characterized by enmity as by cooperation? What kind of "passionately felt community" could they

---

[5] Eben Hezer Sinuraya, personal interview with Mary Steedly.

[6] Anthony Reid, *Imperial Alchemy: Nationalism and Political Identity in Southeast Asia* (Cambridge: Cambridge University Press, 2010), 26.

have imagined? What did independence mean to them? What, in other words, was this strange "alchemy of revolution"?

This is what political scientists refer to as a "puzzle": a seemingly paradoxical situation or event that may serve to illuminate aspects of more general phenomena—in this case, the nature of decolonization, peasant political consciousness, mass violence, and the nationalisms of post-World War II Asia. There is no shortage of possible answers to this puzzle. Resistance "from below" is a well-worn topic in a range of disciplines and places, both historical and contemporary. Slave revolts and peasant uprisings, riots and crowds, millenarian and cargo cults, religious movements, royalist pretenders, supernatural signs and rumors, and prophecies of the "world turned upside down" have all been widely examined, with an equally wide range of explanations: psychological, political-economic, cultural, sociological. In some cases, they are said to be the outcome of external pressures—global economic forces, national or international politics, the intensification of state power—in the absence of intermediary mechanisms capable of alleviating such damages, or the "joint production" of political cleavages at the national and local level. In others, the explanation is located in the psychic disruptions of colonialism, the anxieties of modernity, the collapse of state authority, the contradictions of capitalist exploitation, the misconstrued message of Christian missions, or any of a range of other forces.

You could say that there are too many explanations here rather than too few, so that it is possible to select from the menu of options and find an explanatory fit in virtually any given case, and many of these can be applied, at least in part, to the Karo case. But where a political scientist might aim to solve the puzzle of popular mobilization in Karoland, I want to retain a sense of puzzlement, to use it as a guide in tracking both the unaccounted-for events of the Independence struggle, and the memories and stories that have been produced around them. This means regarding stories as more than just sites for information retrieval or strategic positioning. It means attending to their form as well as content, to the shape that memory takes in narrative, to the layers of interpretation through which it is pressed, the way it circles and circulates, how it escapes, is recaptured, and escapes again—or doesn't.

In this, I align myself, at least halfway, with Benedict Anderson's magisterial *Imagined Communities*, which argues that nations and nationalisms are "cultural artifacts." "To understand them properly," he argues, "we need to consider carefully how they have come into historical being, in what ways their meanings have changed over time, and why, today, they command such profound emotional legitimacy."[7] As is well known, Anderson identifies the source of nationalist thought in a "complex 'crossing' of discrete historical forces" in eighteenth century Europe. These forces include the decline of monarchy, the rise of print-capitalism, and the emergence of a concept of temporal simultaneity, or "homogenous, empty time."[8] This conceptual platform could then be transplanted, in "modular" form, to "a great many social terrains," most notably via the "last wave" nationalisms of Europe's colonial empires in the second half of the twentieth century.[9]

---

[7] Anderson, *Imagined Communities*, 4.
[8] Anderson, *Imagined Communities*, 4.
[9] Anderson, *Imagined Communities*, 4, 113.

Anderson lays out a plausible case for the origins and spread of the *idea* of nationalism—how, for instance, the concept of the nation could appear to political philosophers, scholars, and movement leaders—but stops short of accounting for the willingness of an entire population, especially those situated on the nation's outskirts, "not so much to kill, as willingly to die for such limited imaginings."[10] How, in short, does nationalism "catch on" in the first place, not just as an intellectual project but as a deeply felt reality, a community of "attachments," of shared being and belonging, especially among those who are perhaps not readers of newspapers or novels, or not among the "tender pilgrims" moving up the educational or administrative pyramid of the colonial state?[11]

Here I want to approach these issues via a peculiar subset of Karo narratives that display what I—somewhat playfully—have described as "culinary nationalism." That is, these are stories that use food as an idiom to communicate, display, disturb, or limit the extent of national belonging or communal imagining. Karo stories about food could be patriotic or grotesque; they could be a measure of self-sacrifice, shared hardship, or self-interest; they could expand the limits of sociality or signify a world turned upside down. One thing that made them interesting to me is that, like most of the stories about the Independence struggle that I collected, they didn't contradict, but neither did they exactly coincide with official histories of the struggle. I'm going to present a range of these accounts, then turn in the end to a brief discussion of their broader implications for theories of nationalism, in particular for such top-down, textually based models as *Imagined Communities*. But first, I want to take a detour into the art of ethnographic listening. Appropriately, it takes the form of a story. (And here's where the elephant comes in.)

• • •

"But like now, say, which would taste better, elephant meat or beef?" Laughter cut through the heavy air like a breeze from the mountains. It was mid-afternoon, when the Sitepu household usually drowsed in the muggy lowland heat, before a round of cool baths and fresh clothes refreshed us for dinner, outings, or evening visitors. The voices seemed to be coming from the "project office" we had set up in an unused, windowless study at the front of the house. Two large desks were squeezed into the tiny space, and two computers set up for transcribing interviews. With a couple of chairs, a printer, two cheap tape recorders for transcribing interviews, my cameras and recording equipment, boxes of audio and video cassettes, and a rotating fan that just barely moved the heavy air, there was hardly room for anyone to squeeze in, let alone the five people I found there.

My adopted sisters Cici and Nova were hard at work, with their younger sister Ninin, their cousin Helmi, and my assistant Fariana tucked up on the floor. *"What's so funny?"* I asked, poking my head in the doorway. *"Hey Sis,"* Cici responded casually. *"It's nothing. We're just working on this interview."* A few more giggles percolated up from the floor. Cici slipped her headphones back on. Almost immediately she cried, *"Oh, no, she's doing it again!"* Then, after a pause, *"Sis, who is this person? Why did you let her hijack your interview like that?"* She rewound the tape and unplugged her

---
[10] Anderson, *Imagined Communities*, 7.
[11] Anderson, *Imagined Communities*, 121, 141.

headphones. *"Listen to this."* A girl's voice rolled tinnily from the tape recorder's small speakers: *"So is that the only way to kill an elephant?"* They all shrieked with laughter again.

I remembered the interview well. It was with a woman by the name of Nandé Wajib, who had worked as a nurse in the Gunung Setember field hospital in a forested area near the Karo district border.[12] Ninin and I had gone alone to her place just outside Medan because none of our usual crew had been free that afternoon. A teenage girl was staying with her at the time, a niece or maybe a granddaughter, who joined us during the course of the interview. I didn't write down her real name, but will, for expository purposes, call her Sungkun Berita, "Asking for News."[13] Relatives, neighbors, and passers-by, young and old, often sat in on our interviews, and sometimes they would ask a question or two of their own. I usually welcomed these uninvited audiences. Karo storytelling is an interlocutionary event, in which listeners' questions, comments, and emphatic echoes of lines of dialogue push the action forward, call for elaboration of details in a conventionally spare plot line, or even create an opening for another story. These audiences created a comfortable and stimulating context for storytelling, provoked recollection, and gave us a sense of which topics excited interest and which were considered uninteresting, inappropriate, or irrelevant. They kept the conversation going, and sometimes probed for details we wouldn't have known to ask about.

Not everyone was an equally skilled interlocutor, however. Nova and Cici, who were trained, respectively, in the practical sciences of agronomy and engineering, complained that Sungkun Berita's questions were just "random" (I., *sembarangan*). *How could someone get run over by a tank?* she asked. *Couldn't they get out of the way? Don't tanks have brakes? How many people did the hospital hold? Where did the medicines come from? Didn't you get paid? How does elephant meat taste? Is that the only way to kill an elephant?* Rather than facilitating the flow of narration, inquiries like these blocked (or, as Cici said, "hijacked") it. Ironically, the more interested she was in a subject, the more questions she asked. By this measure, it was the story of Nandé Wajib's encounter with the elephant that most thoroughly captured her imagination.

• • •

Nandé Wajib: *One time we did have a chance to eat meat, because this soldier shot an elephant, there was an elephant that was shot. They just roasted the elephant meat* [on a fire]. *When the elephant came, this guy waited for it. If the elephant spotted us, we'd be dead from him chasing us. So several people got ready.*

Sungkun Berita: *How did they kill it?*

Nandé Wajib: *Shot it.*

Sungkun Berita: *If it's shot is it sure to die?*

---

[12] Tapes were identified at the time of the interview with a numerical code based on the date. Informants' names were recorded separately and not available to my transcribers. This was not a perfect security system, but there was little need for one.

[13] "Sungkun Berita" is the title of one of the segments of *Lima puluh kurang dua*, the great piece of Karo music.

Nandé Wajib: *Yeah, if it's hit, you can kill it. It was killed, but its baby wasn't killed. The baby lay there beside its mama. We felt sorry for it, a newborn baby from the look of it, but as big as the biggest ox. Meaning that even though it's not small it had just been born. So its dead mama was just lying there, it was standing beside her. They cut it up, divided the meat with the local people …*

Sungkun Berita: *Didn't the baby get mad?*

Nandé Wajib: *What did he know about getting mad, he was still little. So the baby was cut up, too. The baby's meat was tastier than the mother's. Because the, what do you call them, the elephant's tendons are really big.*

Sungkun Berita: *Was the elephant meat tasty?*

Nandé Wajib: *Good enough, it was like beef.*

Me [Mary Steedly]: *If you've been eating nothing but yams, well, it's tasty, right?*

Nandé Wajib: *It was good enough.*

Sungkun Berita: *But now, compared to now, which tastes better, elephant meat or beef?*

Nandé Wajib: *Beef is better. How could an elephant be good to eat, because elephants work hard. Whenever they pass by, you know,* soouu *… that's the sound they make. Not just one of them passes by. They travel in big groups. So if they go by, or if we know they want to go by, because their sound is really strong. So those people waited for them.*

Sungkun Berita: *So what do you do when they go by?*

Nandé Wajib: *You hide! If they catch your scent, they'll chase you. When they run, they run like this, they go straight ahead like this. They go on straight for a long way. Then they turn around, straight again. So if you want to get away from them, you've got to dodge over there. If you run like this* [straight ahead], *they'll chase you till they catch you. That's not the way to get away from them.*

Sungkun Berita: *Cut across* [their path], *right?*

Nandé Wajib: *Yeah, crossways. If we see they're running over that way, we go the other way. Don't run straight, because with elephants, they run straight.*

Sungkun Berita: *So, running around in circles, how about that? They can't do that, right?*

Nandé Wajib: *They can't do it, because they're so big. So they can't turn in circles, they just run straight, a long way, then they come back, that's how we can get away from them. But once there was a man who said, he couldn't get away from them anymore because he was cut up with razor grass, because it was all underbrush, all woods. Well, it was "guerrilla style," we were in the forest, you know. In the forest, how could you keep anything clean? There were lots of chili plants in the woods. That's how it was there.*

Sungkun Berita: *So the elephant meat was divided up with the people who lived there, right?*

Nandé Wajib: *Yeah, we shared it with them. One* tumba [basket, small bushel] *per household. Sometimes if it was a big family, they gave them two* tumbas.

Sungkun Berita: *So that's the only way to kill an elephant.*

Nandé Wajib: *Yeah, shoot them. Dead, she fell, the others all ran away, well, they were startled, you know. She was dead.*

Sungkun Berita: *So you shoot from two directions?*

Nandé Wajib: *One direction. If you shoot from two directions, well, you might hit each other. Shoot like this, well, one could miss the target. If everyone shoots at once from here, then he might fall with a crash, because of that he'll crash down. We didn't do it from two directions. From this one direction.*

Sungkun Berita: *When the elephant was killed, how many people were shooting?*

Nandé Wajib: *That day, maybe five people, I don't remember too well.*

Sungkun Berita: *That's when you finally got to eat meat. A big celebration, huh?*

Nandé Wajib: *Yeah, otherwise, there wasn't any at all.*

Near the interview's end, Sungkun Berita tried to recapture the frisson of dangerous encounters and strange foods by asking whether they had ever eaten snake meat. *"No, never,"* replied Nandé Wajib firmly. *"Why in the world would we eat snake? Oh no!"*

• • •

I sometimes thought that a Karo history of the Independence struggle could be constructed entirely from stories about food, so frequently did they occur in our interviews. Stories about food illuminated commitments to the nationalist cause and lapses in military discipline, the expansive reach of hospitality, the struggles of displacement, the limits of social personhood, and the disorder of a time out of joint. They shorthanded a sense of shared privation, marked the boundaries of community, or keyed in a mood of wartime nostalgia. They grounded concepts like patriotism, sacrifice, and community in memories of concrete, sensuous experience—the taste of a saltless meal, the toughness of meat, the color of rice, the labor of meal preparation—making them, in the process, something shared and deeply felt. Just about anything that happened could be given extra narrative weight by associating it with food, and whenever food was mentioned you could be sure that you were being told something important. (As Nandé Wajib's story of the elephant suggests, they [important narratives] could also be "hijacked" by the interests and attentions of a present-day audience—often in ways more subtle than Sungkun Berita's persistent questioning.)

People reflecting on hard times have a lot to say about what there was to eat, how it was gotten, who was generous, and who was not. Karo women, who were responsible for most of the farming and cooking even in ordinary circumstances, put particular emphasis on the gathering, preparing, and sharing of food. And while food is not ordinarily a topic of much interest either in everyday Karo conversation or in the legends and folktales that comprise a local history of Karo social life, the sharing of food plays a large part in the delineation of kinship roles and statuses as well as in broader notions of hospitality and generosity. So it was not particularly surprising that Karo men and women staged the moral lessons of Independence in terms of the making and sharing of food. In stories of the Japanese occupation, for instance, the unequal distribution of food exposes the hollowness of Japanese claims of brotherhood: *"We called [the Japanese] our older brothers,"* schoolteacher Muham told us, but in the end *"they kept the good rice, we got the yams."* Here's how bad it was, Nandé Timur complained. The Japanese fed rice to the pigs and forced toothless elders to eat coarse, hard feed corn, or even birdseed. Lenggang Bangun went to volunteer for Japanese military training, but realized that their promises of liberation were false when he saw Indonesian officer trainees reduced to eating dirty pumpkin, laid on the ground, chopped up with a machete, and served on a piece of coconut shell.[14]

In contrast to accounts of the hardship and deprivation of Japanese Time, women's stories of the beginning of Independence revel in abundance. In them, the giving and preparation of food is a sign of patriotic commitment. Schoolteacher 'Cik Muham, who was an ardent nationalist propagandist, quoted one of her speeches to us: *"Give us rice to feed our soldiers,"* she said. *"Otherwise, how will our soldiers eat? If there are tomatoes, peppers, vegetables, onions in your fields, bring them here … So our soldiers at the front lines don't have to go hungry."* Everyone was happy to give, *"even if all their rice went to feed the soldiers"*:

> At the beginning of Independence, everything was tough. There was no money, nothing. Even bullets, you know, the only way to get them was by stealing. There was just nothing. Only spirit that was brimming over. In terms of spirit, there was no one who mumbled, no one who grumbled, everyone was happy, even if all their rice went to feed the soldiers. Tomatoes, peppers, whatever there was in the village, they gave it all to feed the soldiers. Yeah, all of them helped like that.

Nandé Madasa beru Ginting recalled the work that village girls had to do when soldiers came to the village:

> Back then there wasn't any rice. We'd all beg for rice at all the houses, one would give two *tumbas*, three *tumbas*, like that at the beginning of Independence, to feed those who found the enemy. Then, pound it at night, even at night you'd pound it. So then, when someone came, called, the ones who were to be fed, you'd ask for rice at the houses, there wasn't any husked rice, there wasn't a mill. Pound it, pound it like that, then cook it. We wouldn't get to sleep before dawn if someone came who hadn't been fed. So then, what to fix to go with it? If nothing was cooked, you'd go get something from the house again. Well, pound the rice, make the stew. Nothing was off limits. You'd catch somebody's chicken, or somebody's pig, they weren't off limits.

"Did you know these soldiers, granny? Were they from around here?" my assistant Jabatin asked. *"They were from other places,"* she said. *"If they were from around here, well, wouldn't we know them already, know how we were related to them?"* She meant that if the soldiers had been related, however distantly, to anyone in the village, then it would have been up to their local kinfolk to feed and house them. *"Sometimes they said the ones to be fed came from Medan. We didn't even know them, we didn't have the chance to find out*

---

[14] Spinning the privations of the Japanese occupation in a different direction, Piah Manik describes in detail the meager farewell meal she prepared for departing Heiho recruits—rice mixed with yams and curried goat intestines—to demonstrate her family's commitment to hospitality even in such a time of general hardship and scarcity, thus sidestepping the more morally ambiguous issue of her father's culpability as a Heiho recruiter and Japanese collaborator.

how they were related. What else could you do? Soon they'd move on to someplace else. That was the problem. Tomorrow others would come, too."

In Nandé Madasa's account, the flood of transient and undifferentiated freedom fighters becomes the narrative condition for an idealized depiction of communal harmony and generosity. Karo are obliged by social practice and by custom to take care of even the most distant of kin, but here kinship doesn't matter, and no one's livestock is "off limits"—whoever comes should be fed. Nor is the feeding of the soldiers from elsewhere an occasional or extraordinary occurrence; it is what happens, seemingly, every day: "Tomorrow others would come, too." The designation of these soldiers as neither relatives nor nonrelatives marks them as extraordinary and the food they receive as freely given.

The moral significance of food is clear in accounts like these, in which the national community is not so much imagined as it is instantiated through face-to-face practices of generosity and hospitality (or, in the case of stories of Japanese Time, the inverse of such practices taught people "how it feels to be colonized"). Soldiers who were the beneficiaries of village hospitality sometimes had different stories to tell, qualifying the virtue of village generosity with its tendency toward parochial thinking. One man noted, for instance, that soldiers stationed near a village might not be fed if they didn't engage with the enemy: *"If we didn't fight, they would get stubborn, and finally they wouldn't give us anything to eat. So at a minimum we had to fight once in every three days ... We had to run around looking for fights."* Another told how he had gotten in trouble with his commanding officer when well-meaning villagers repeatedly served pork to a squad of Muslim Acehnese fighters, who deserted their posts in disgust over this treatment: *"It wasn't my fault,"* he explained. *"It was the fault of the villagers' not understanding."* Another soldier—this one himself Acehnese—recounted with patronizing humor some of the strange food items he and his troops encountered in Karoland: *cipera*, a cornmeal gravy that *"looked just like your morning shit,"* a resemblance enhanced by its being served in what appeared to be a chamber pot; *teritis*, a stew made of the partly digested contents of a cow's rumen, which *"absolutely could not be eaten"*; and *bohan*, seasoned congealed blood roasted in bamboo tubes, which provoked the bemused response, *"Different fields, different grasshoppers, there certainly are a variety of traditional foods that can be found in our Nation."*[15]

One of the most common food stories told by soldiers had to do with the red rice of the Medan "front"—the term used for the nationalist militia encampments blockading the lowland capital. *"Now I'm going to tell you something I'll bet you've never heard before,"* said Bapa Ruth Ginting, our sometime travel guide, reflecting on his time at the front. *"The rice they gave us at the front, it was red! It was wrapped in teak leaves, you see, each portion, and the leaves stained the rice. They turned it red. That's what I remember about the food at the front."* Bapa Ruth's claim to originality notwithstanding, just about every Karo man who served in the popular militias mentioned the red rice of the Medan front to us. It was a sensuous hook that seemed to capture the essence of life at the front: a mix of estrangement and routine that could cast a defamiliarizing glare on something as ordinary as a packaged meal of rice. No doubt their rice wasn't always

---

[15] Haji R. Sjahnan, *Dari Medan Area Ke Pedalaman Dan Kembali Ke-Kota Medan* (Medan: Dinas Sejarah Kodam-II/BB, 1982), 134.

red, though the former soldiers, in a rush of nostalgic remembrance, recalled it that way.

Medan's streetside vendors and food shops commonly served (and many still do) individual meals wrapped in banana leaves, but because of the number of servings that had to be prepared every day for the soldiers at the front, alternative wrappers had to be found. When the teak trees that lined the main highway to the city were cut down to block the road, their large leaves were put to use in the public kitchens where soldiers' meals were prepared. The kitchens were overseen by staff officers or, more often, by their wives. Karo girls from nearby villages sometimes helped out, but most of the work was done by Javanese estate laborers. They cooked the rice, topped it with boiled cassava leaves or stews made with vegetables trucked down from the highlands, and folded each individual portion in a leaf wrapper. Militia leaders notified the kitchen staff of their unit's position and current strength (which varied considerably from day to day), and the correct number of ready-made meals would be delivered to them.

The unexpected redness of the soldiers' rice contains, but does not draw attention to, this entire backstage apparatus of food collection, preparation, and distribution, which linked uplands and lowlands, home front and front lines, the labor of women and the battles of men. It also hints at but does not display other less attractive aspects of military mobilization, such as the exploitation of plantation laborers, crop levies on farmers, appropriations and downright theft of property from civilians, political infighting, and competition between armed units over strategic resources. These are subsumed by the nostalgic pleasures of sensuous recollection, the minor strangenesses of wartime experience, and the triumph of military discipline over civilian disorder that is the basis of Indonesia's contemporary "culture of violence."

When it comes to the military campaigns of the *Revolusi Fisik* ("physical revolution," a term that distinguishes the actual period of fighting against the Dutch from the internal violence of the 1946 "social revolution") and particularly the evacuation of the highlands as Dutch troops swept through the region, Karo stories about food take on an unsettled, anxious tone. In these stories, food is not something you can count on.

The evacuation has become an iconic moment in the Karo social imaginary, in which it signals a profound break with the past and a first step in the move to modernity. It was a time of traveling in unfamiliar, often dangerous places; of encountering strangers and being compelled to adapt to their ways; of coping with scarcity, uncertainty, terror, and unpredictable violence. Villages were burned, either by their inhabitants or by popular militias or, in some cases, by Dutch military units. It was a time when communities were scattered *bagi cingkeru irambasken*, "like Job's Tears [a plant] when it's beaten,"[16] and life passages—marriage, death, birth—could not be celebrated or commemorated in the customary way. Stories of this time reflect on the human condition in extreme circumstances: when hospitality fails, strangeness is commonplace, and the requirements of sociality are unmanageable. Seemingly trivial

---

[16] The reference is to the seed head of Job's Tears, a variety of grass. When the plant is struck against a wall or stone, the seeds scatter in all directions, "scattering the scattered," as Masri Singarimbun puts it, e.g., "Said of a scattered position, for example, the spread of people during the evacuation." See Masri Singarimbun, *Kinship, Descent and Alliance among the Karo Batak* (Berkeley: University of California Press, 1975), 168.

matters take on an added weight. Food was strange, uncanny, unsavory—not quite fit for human consumption. *"No salt,"* Karo said, referencing the salt embargo set up by the Dutch, and describing how food had no taste without it. *"We ate* béwan," people told me over and over. *"You know what* béwan *is, don't you?"* Then they would describe this hardy weed—how it looks, how it has to be cooked, what it tastes like. These experiences were shared and, when they came up (as they almost always did) in group conversations, everyone would nod knowingly, *"yes, that's right, we did that too. That's just how it was."* Evacuees told stories of having to flee Dutch attacks while their rice was half cooked—*"we took it off the fire and ran away. We ate it just like that, and it seemed good to us. If you're hungry enough!"*—or of arriving in villages where the refugees were not even allowed to borrow a spice mortar to prepare their meals.

Sometimes these stories go further, unsettling the boundaries between the human and natural worlds. Nandé Wajib's story of eating the elephant, despite the fact-finding efforts of her audience (*"which tastes better, elephant meat or beef?"*), dwells on the pathos of mother and baby killed together. *"We felt sorry for it* [the baby elephant]."

Nandé Timur, who had also been at the Gunung Setember hospital, told a different version of the story about the killing of the elephant. She didn't mention the baby, instead focusing on how this act had unsettled the natural order:

> Nandé Timur: *Elephant, we even ate elephant.*
>
> Me: *At Gunung Setember?*
>
> Nandé Timur: *Right. It was really tough. It was shot, right? It was shot. So then, it was divided up. One day, we cooked it all day, and it still wasn't soft. You couldn't cut it, that elephant. You couldn't eat it. It wasn't edible. It was really bitter! Then because it was dead, you know, the elephant, we were attacked by ... mosquitoes! At that time. They were brought, the elephants brought the mosquitoes into the village. It was like bees, the sound of the mosquitoes, because it was dead. The elephant.*

Another story that unsettled the human/natural distinction was told by Nandé Riah, the wife of a militia commander who spent nearly a year in a jungle camp near the village of Lau Primbon.

> There was a fellow in Lau Primbon who butchered a goat. They brought some meat, so then, eh, what are you carrying, we said, meat. We all ripped that meat up, we didn't roast it, we didn't grill it. We ate it just like that, that's why if you haven't seen meat in a while, you know, you're, um ... Raw goat meat, we ate it right up. Because there wasn't anything to eat there. Well, roast it first, no way. No time to start a fire to roast the meat, we ate it blood and all. That's what happens when you're in the forest too long. We hadn't eaten meat or anything.

I could go on with stories like these—of humans acting like animals, or animals regarded as quasi-human, of the hospitality that joins people in society disregarded or, perhaps worse, enacted but with fatal effects. But let me turn to my conclusion.

• • •

When Karo women and men responded to the "gong of independence" in 1945, they did so in ways that had little, if anything, to do with "Indonesia" as a historically given national entity or even as a conceptually useful political object. The kind of community they imagined had to do with more intimate forms of comradeship, equality, and social justice, frequently exemplified in the sharing of food.

Memory, as Maurice Halbwachs says, is an effect of community.[17] It is constructed in dialogue, activated by interrogation, and framed by the conventions of narrative plausibility. Personal memory may be constricted by official limits on public discourse, by the formal shape of public commemoration and rituals of remembrance, or by the lack of an interested or knowledgeable audience. But you could just as easily say that community is an effect of memory. The sense of national belonging in Karoland was neither the source nor the outcome of common experiences—of hardship and aspiration, mobilization, evacuation, violence, or homecoming. Still less was it an already-existing structure of feeling, recognized or interpellating. Rather, it came about through the sharing of stories ("memory of the body"). The eating of *béwan* or the taste of a saltless meal does not in itself generate a sense of collective identity, but the recognition of the commonality of these experiences may do so.

I've spoken here about what I call the "memory of the senses" to point to a certain powerful mode of recollection. Memory attaches itself most intensely to sensory experience: taste, for instance, as I have described here, but also sight and sound, bodily states, smells. These are often small elements that evoke broader structures of feeling and remembrance. Even if the stories wrapped around them differ, a vivid, shared sense-memory can provoke a kind of collusive bonding. "That's just how it was," people said. "We did that, too."

Karo nationalism, in this sense, had no beginning; it emerged "halfway on," or after the fact, as people shared stories of things that had happened to them during the struggle for independence. Food, which engages the senses directly, but also carries a range of implicit social meanings—is a perfect vehicle for imagining the expanse as well as the limits of a community, whether it be national, ethnic, local, or, indeed, universal. But it was not the only one. Gender and sexuality, physical labor and bodily discipline or training, the extent of travels and the sense of place, acts of violence and their tangible and intangible traces, are some of the other sites in which the memory of the nation comes into being.

---

[17] Maurice Halbwachs, *On Collective Memory* (Chicago: University of Chicago Press), 1992.

NARRATIVE

James Peacock

When I first came to know Mary Steedly, she was an enthusiastic student of folklore. While she is rightly known as a scholar of Indonesian history and narrative, many people may not be acquainted with the fieldwork projects that she carried out in North Carolina during her training in the folklore curriculum at the University of North Carolina–Chapel Hill (UNC). The point of these comments is to fill out a formative chapter in Mary's history that predates her well-known work in Sumatra, and to show that throughout all her work we can see her consistent attention to meaning, humanity, and story.

In 1978 and '79, Mary worked on two distinct projects among the Lumbee community in Robeson County, North Carolina. One of these resulted in her 1979 master's thesis on the field study of a healer named Pastor Vernon Cooper.[1] Three advisors' names appear on that thesis: Daniel Patterson, Charles (Terry) Zug, and my own. Mary also became involved in a project on Lumbee religious services at the invitation of her fourth mentor, Ruel Tyson, who was a UNC professor and chair of the religious studies program. In recalling her time at UNC, I have re-read her thesis and some of her fieldnotes, given to me by Tyson. Like the madeleines, the cookies that transported Proust to the past in *Swann's Way*, both sets of documents evoke a host of remembrances. Some of these can help us reconstruct parts of this brief period in Mary's career.[2]

James Peacock is a professor emeritus in the department of anthropology at the University of North Carolina–Chapel Hill, where he was the Kenan Distinguished Professor and director of the Center for International Studies.

[1] Mary Margaret Steedly, "The Evidence of Things Not Seen: Faith and Tradition in a Lumbee Healing Practice" (master's thesis, Curriculum in Folklore, University of North Carolina–Chapel Hill, 1979).

[2] To prepare this tribute I spoke with Ruel Tyson, Daniel Patterson, and a classmate of Mary's from that time, Ken George. Ken and Mary went on to study at the University of Michigan, which launched both in their excellent fieldwork in Indonesia, she in Sumatra and he in Sulawesi. I am particularly grateful to

The UNC folklore program was at the time chaired by Patterson, who recalls Mary as a source of "wit and humanity and curiosity," and whose deep knowledge of verbal and musical expression and meaning among the Shakers of New England and the Primitive Baptists of the Blue Ridge Mountains surely made an impact on her. He was a professor of English along with another of Mary's mentors, Zug. Zug, who earned his folklore doctorate at the University of Pennsylvania and authored *Turners and Burners*, a classic study of North Carolina's great pottery tradition.[3] Tyson, who was trained in hermeneutics at the University of Chicago's Committee on Social Thought, focused on Lumbee Christianity and specialized in the detailed dissection of words.

We may therefore note what Mary received from her study at UNC: mentoring by superb teachers who were also superb scholars, writers, and human beings with a deep appreciation of local culture. What she did not receive at UNC, I infer, was training in Indonesian studies. At the time, I was one of the only faculty members on campus with any experience in Indonesia, but I had had little training in Indonesian studies while at Harvard, and I never taught a course on Indonesia at UNC.[4] I got involved in UNC's folklore program around 1967, when I first arrived, and began teaching a course on symbols that I had started at Princeton University, and which many folklore students took over the years. Patterson and I also did extensive fieldwork together. Hence, I was on Mary's committee not because of my involvement in Indonesia, which she took up after going to the University of Michigan, but because of the convergence of symbols and folklore.

Mary's UNC thesis is a masterpiece of fieldwork, writing, and compassion that foreshadows the brilliance of her later books on Indonesia. As she stated in her thesis abstract, it is "a description of the practice of a single healer, Vernon Cooper, a Lumbee Indian whose work combines traditional herbal lore with healing by faith."[5] In her acknowledgements, Mary thanks Cooper, his family, and his patients, expressing the hope that "this thesis will express in part my admiration and respect for him and his work."[6] She then begins the thesis with a wonderful portrait of the physical and cultural landscape of the Lumbee Indian setting before focusing in on the figure of Cooper himself.

Mary opens with the sentence "Vernon Cooper is a healer." She continues, "I first met Vernon Cooper in April of 1978" and then quotes the account of "Bertha M.," who was healed by Cooper after being in a serious automobile accident: "When I was in intensive care … I told them to call him to pray. I could tell when he prayed … I believe the Lord sent him for this work."[7] Mary goes on to describe how he worked

---

Ruel Tyson for sharing his experiences and documents concerning Mary, especially since he was ill; he passed away several weeks after our final conversations, but was entirely lucid during them.

[3] Charles G. Zug III, *Turners and Burners: The Folk Potters of North Carolina* (Chapel Hill: North Carolina University Press, 1986).

[4] Building on an effort that I launched after returning from Indonesia in 1996, UNC today offers vibrant programming on Southeast Asia as part of its Curriculum in Global Studies. All of this, however, occurred long after Mary's time there.

[5] Steedly, "The Evidence of Things Not Seen," abstract.

[6] Steedly, "The Evidence of Things Not Seen," acknowledgements.

[7] Steedly, "The Evidence of Things Not Seen," 1.

with Bertha and others until she was healed. Later, Mary presents Cooper's life story in his own words:

> When I was near twenty years old I [had the] full responsibility of a family. The way was hard. I was working at Pearson Brothers farm, and at the sawmill, and helping my daddy farm ... life continued to be rough ... Hoover days ... I done more and got less than the average person ... I drove trucks ... The first truck that I drove didn't have any windshield or place to sit down ... [8]

Mary observes, "In talking about himself, Vernon Cooper exhibited the same deliberateness, the search for meaning and sense, which is later found in all his speech and actions ... He is a large man with a strong face ... at 72 he moves and talks slowly." Further down she tells us that Vernon was the oldest of seven children, and notes that "he learned much about herbs from his grandmother and from a homeopathic doctor, Jesse Hair, on whose farm he lived and from whom he learned until his family left the Hair farm and moved to Robeson County."[9] With a close eye to detail, Mary describes Cooper carrying out his work at home, often until midnight, with trucks pulling up and parking outside his yard in order to bring patients to and from his house.

Displaying her developing skill as an ethnographic writer, Mary allows Cooper's voice to resound in her text as a source of both testimony and commentary. After passing on Cooper's statement, "I was called to this work in 1927," Mary notes that "he fought against the call until 1960 after four heart attacks, which he sees as God's warnings about his resisting the call."[10] Further on, she ends her biographical chapter on a bittersweet note, with Cooper first wondering out loud if he is an anachronism and then countering the thought: "'It seems like just something that's negative. But,' he adds, smiling quickly, 'Sometimes you can get a picture out of a negative.'"[11]

Throughout the remainder of the thesis, Mary quotes generously from Cooper's account of himself, capturing his language and philosophies and drawing together his theories and insights into illness and treatment. So gripping is Mary's writing that one becomes enthralled by Cooper's perspectives on the body, illness, and belief.

In her analysis of the context, content, and structure of Vernon Cooper's healing practice, we can see the emergence of Mary's distinctive and eclectic approach to theory and ethnography. She draws on anthropological studies of symbols and classification systems, citing classics by Marcel Mauss, Émile Durkheim, and Claude Lévi-Strauss, and appending a detailed chart of terms and categories that documents Cooper's approach to healing conditions caused by unseen forces. While she cites ethnographic studies of the Lumbee by Karen Blu and Gerald Sider,[12] she does *not* cite

---

[8] Steedly, "The Evidence of Things Not Seen," 27.
[9] Steedly, "The Evidence of Things Not Seen," 28.
[10] Steedly, "The Evidence of Things Not Seen," 32–34.
[11] Steedly, "The Evidence of Things Not Seen," 32–34.
[12] See: Karen Blu, "Varieties of Ethnic Identity: Anglo-Saxons, Blacks, Indians, and Jews in a Southern County," *Ethnicity* 4 (1977): 263–86; Karen Blu, "We People: Understanding Lumbee Indian Identity in a Tri-Racial Situation" (Ph.D. dissertation, University of Chicago, 1972); and Gerald Marc Sider, "A Political History of the Lumbee Indians of Robeson County, North Carolina: A Case Study of Ethnic Political Affiliations" (Ph.D. dissertation, New School for Social Research, 1971).

William Pollitzer's genetic studies, which attempted to explain the wide range of phenotypes in Lumbee families. Nor does she draw on recordings and descriptions of Lumbee religious services with the intent of comparing them, as another folklorist might have done, to African American and white Pentecostals in the Piedmont counties. Instead, her focus rests primarily on the central figure of Cooper, the healer.

Mary's representation of Cooper combines two genres: life history, and what Mauss and Lévi-Strauss would term "classification" or "*la pensée sauvage*," the difference being that Mary not only conveys Cooper's "native" categories of thought, but expands them into an account of his worldview. Thus, alongside an extensive chart of the key terms that explain Cooper's system of healing and illness, Mary offers a discursive account of his pluralistic Christian, medical, and ethno-scientific outlook, couched in his own language. The effect is as engaging as if one were reading a novelist's rendition of an almost heroic character in monologue or in dialogue with another character, in this instance, Mary herself. So deeply drawn in as to imagine oneself under the healer's treatment, the reader comes away with admiration and a liking for him. At once precise and absorbing, I find Mary's portrait of Cooper to be one of the most compelling accounts of an individual in all of anthropological (or any other) literature.

It may be noted that in the intervening decades since Mary's research, several members of the Lumbee community have confirmed that Pastor Cooper (his real name) was beloved across the Lumbee region. After becoming national intellectual figures, some Lumbee have turned to the study of their own culture and history in the footsteps of the outsiders who first analyzed their communities—much as Mary herself came to do toward the end of her life.[13]

Another component of Mary's Lumbee fieldwork, as mentioned above, was the work that she carried out as research assistant to Tyson. He recently shared with me a copy of her fieldnotes documenting a service led at Shannon Pentecostal Church, in Robeson County, by Pastor Montana Locklear, a stout, short, dynamo of a man whom I knew as well. Her notes are prefaced by points about meaning, problems, and significance. First, she poses a number of framing questions. What is the meaning of raised arms during worship and what is the visual correlate of verbal testimonies? Second, what problems does Reverend Locklear address? How does he confront the meaning of a recent car accident that had killed an entire family? How does he handle the dedication of an illegitimate child?

These prefatory questions are followed by a verbatim transcription of a single service, further accompanied by a video recording of the same. There is, as well, a commentary in Mary's precise handwriting that shows the attention to detail for which her Indonesia research later came to be known. She describes, for instance, how Reverend Locklear dealt with his congregation when an unsaved mother came forth for the dedication to God of her illegitimate child. The congregation's disapproval was

---

[13] I note in particular Melissa Lowry, who earned her doctorate at Harvard, and David Lowry, who worked with Jean Jackson at MIT and wrote a dissertation on Lumbee missionaries abroad. Melissa is now a professor at UNC and head of the Center for the Study of the American South, while David is on the faculty of Biola University, in California.

made clear as only two congregants came forward when Montana invited the women present to pray for the baby:

> Sister Revels and another older woman (who I recall as being very kind to me). Montana insists that two others come forward. Tableau: Montana, in green with bright tie holding very gently the sleeping infant, dark skin and hair against large white blanket. Young girl in dark blouse and white skirt, standing very straight, head bowed slightly ... [14]

She goes on to describe Bobby and Frances Lowry singing at the pulpit, both crying, adding that while this was not unusual for Frances, it was rather more so for stoic Bobby.

When I spoke with Tyson, he shared with me a vivid comment made by Reverend Locklear on that occasion. As Mary and Tyson were setting up their bulky video camera on a tripod, Locklear remarked, "The brother professor thinks he can record the Holy Ghost!" This was a brilliant comment, I think, about participant observation, and especially about the ethnographic limits to beholding belief. Mary may or may not have thought that she could record the holy ghost, but her field notes demonstrate the careful craftsmanship with which she recorded what she saw and heard. She shared this carefulness with Tyson and Patterson, both of whom were meticulous analysts of what people said and sang in religious contexts, and she remained fascinated by the relationship between seeing, believing, and documenting long after she left North Carolina.

Later in 1979, Tyson and I were working closely together alongside Patterson and his wife, Beverly Bush Patterson, on a separate project encompassing Primitive Baptists as well as black, white, and Lumbee Pentecostals in North Carolina and Virginia. My partnership with Tyson was similar to his and Mary's working relationship in one important respect. Like Mary, I took the wheel as we traveled to observe and record services and interviews. While driving and doing fieldwork, I learned much from Tyson's meticulous memory of any detail, from directions in the complicated, unmarked mountain roads to penetrating issues of theology that went far beyond my own level of interpretation. Years later, Tyson published an outstanding essay entitled "The Testimony of Sister Annie Mae," based on his fieldwork among Lumbee Pentecostals.[15] I have found myself wondering recently how much that essay might owe to Mary. How far was it shaped by a collaboration between two gifted ethnographers with differing backgrounds, ages, genders, and training? I put this question to Tyson. As he recollects it, the material for the essay had actually been gathered with me in 1980, by which time Mary had moved on to other work. Regardless of the chronology, Mary's work with Tyson undoubtedly enriched his own work as well as all of ours, directly as well as obliquely.[16]

---

[14] Mary Steedly's fieldnotes.

[15] Ruel Tyson, "The Testimony of Sister Annie Mae," in *Diversities of Gifts: Field Studies in Southern Religion*, ed. Ruel Tyson, James Peacock, and Daniel Patterson (Champaign: University of Illinois Press, 1988), 105–25.

[16] The funding that framed Mary's and Ruel Tyson's fieldwork deserves to be acknowledged. One project was a study of two major streams of Protestantism in the US South: Calvinism and Pentecostalism. The other was of various movements both inside and outside the United States. The NEH (National Endowment for Humanities) was the main funder of the first, whose principal investigators were James

Turning back to Mary's time in Chapel Hill, we can now broadly surmise about what she received and what she gave in turn. What she received, perhaps, came from superb scholars like Tyson and Patterson: a deep and generous understanding of cultural creation—religious, literary, musical, human. What she gave is evidenced by the presence of this element, broadened and deepened, in her profound and beautiful studies in Indonesia and beyond.

Mary's intellectual path would unwittingly parallel my own. During her time in North Carolina, I could not have known that her doctoral work would soon take her to Indonesia, my own first field site, or that her later research would bring her back to the southern United States, much as mine did. Yet, in retrospect, we can see much consistency in her development. Her earliest work in North Carolina demonstrated a curiosity for the invisible, an interest in documentation, and a gift for conveying details even when they did not conform to the story. These later came to be among the theoretical hallmarks for which she will be remembered. It is moving to see these qualities in her early field notes, to know that her gifts for combining sensitive, detailed description with broader symbolic analysis were already evident then. We can be grateful for what she learned and what she gave as she moved beyond that short time in that place.

Peacock, Ruel Tyson, and Dan Patterson. The NIH (National Institutes of Health) funded the second, and the principal investigators were Terrence Evens and James Peacock. Mary worked with Tyson and Peacock on the first project in 1980, and with Peacock on the second.

TELLTALE

Patricia Spyer

"Telltale" is my word. It gathers some of the ways in which I want to remember and honor Mary. Telltale speaks to the acute attention and thinking that she brought to her work, to the subtlety, nuance, power, and persuasiveness of her writing, and to the way I imagine many Indonesianists and other scholars will continue to recall and draw on her insights and contributions for years to come. Telltale evokes Mary's method and the pleasure of surprise and sense of adventure that she found in her fieldwork and ethnography. Telltale conjures the talebearer or teller of tales, a figure who moves in and out of Mary's writing—in the guise of the memory artist from her masterful *Rifle Reports*,[1] or the elusive spirits whose oblique voices intervene occasionally from the margins of everyday urbanity in North Sumatra's bustling metropolis Medan to lend shape to the sociality, ritual, and narrative experience at the heart of *Hanging without a Rope*.[2]

Mary had a keen alertness to the telltale in the sense of an outward sign, an indication of something, however slight, that marks a difference, discloses a possibility, intimates a shift in direction. Occasionally, something telltale clamors for attention. More often, it is small, even modest in its singularity, a telling detail that stands out from its surroundings, gives pause, catches the eye, makes one listen more closely or look again. Telltale assumes myriad forms—a word, a gesture, a tone, a silence, a change of posture, something scuttling at the edge of the visual field. Telltale is not just noticeable but suggestive, since it betrays the presence of something else—another way of telling, someone else speaking, or a fugitive site of ephemerality—a concept to which I will have occasion to return.

Patricia Spyer is a professor of anthropology at the Graduate Institute, Geneva, Switzerland.

[1] Mary Margaret Steedly, *Rifle Reports: A Story of Indonesian Independence* (Berkeley: University of California Press, 2013).

[2] Mary Margaret Steedly, *Hanging without a Rope: Narrative Experience in Colonial and Postcolonial Karoland* (Princeton: Princeton University Press, 1993).

Mary's engagement with narrated experience in the many forms and genres it presents itself in past and present Karoland is something that not only enriches but also distinguishes the ethnography of her books and other publications. It also accounts for the extraordinary sense of vitality and intimacy of her writing. Many of us, not surprisingly, will remember Mary for the gifted storyteller that she was. Her description of the storytelling artistry of her informant Pak Tua could apply just as well to herself:

> What you need most for telling a story, Pak Tua said, is time. You can't rush a story. You have to go back, repeat, detour, go back again. Pak Tua makes a story like a fisherman makes a net—a knot here, twist to the side, follow this line and that, bring them together. There are long digressions: in the story someone drops an axe, and Pak Tua has to tell you how that axe is made, and the proper way to use it, how the cut and the felling of the tree fit into a larger pattern of events and how one reads the future in the tree's falling, how the tree felled becomes part of a house, how the house becomes a part of the world. Only then can the axe be picked up again.[3]

In his famous essay "The Storyteller," which was one of Mary's favorites, Walter Benjamin laments what he sees as storytelling's demise, exemplified by the traumatized soldiers returning from the First World War's devastating battle fields "poorer in communicable experience."[4] In Chapter 7 of *Hanging without a Rope*, Mary cites Benjamin's observation that "in every case the storyteller is a man who has counsel for his readers," or, in Karoland, for the most part, her listeners.[5] But she departs from Benjamin's conclusion regarding the displacement of storytelling by mere information, asking instead what sort of counsel can be offered in the kind of world lived by, for instance, Pak Tua, an aged former company commander of the Barisan Harimau Liar, the "Wild Tiger Brigade," of Karoland's independence struggle.[6]

No matter how slight and, perhaps, so minute that it risks being disregarded, something telltale may still wield considerable power. This is so when it compels people to take cognizance of something unexpected, invites them to think anew or act differently, or because, in its very smallness, the telltale has the capacity to subsume an idea or gesture to its opposite, to something much larger or momentous than itself. Mary was, of course, aware of this. Writing of the media ghosts she investigates in her contribution to *Images That Move*, she reflects on why horror movies generate the kind of affect they do on audiences. Hauntings haunt, in part, she suggests, because they disavow full presence, relying for their effect on dread or "the anticipation of the worst thing that could possibly happen." This is why effective horror films "defer the moment of ghostly apparition as long as possible, giving the audience only fragmentary glimpses, hints of spectral presence: a distant song, a wisp of long white

---

[3] Steedly, *Hanging without a Rope*, 204.
[4] Benjamin, quoted in Steedly, *Hanging without a Rope*, 209.
[5] Benjamin, quoted in Steedly, *Hanging without a Rope*, 207.
[6] Steedly, *Hanging without a Rope*, 207.

hair, a strange hoof-like foot, a claw-like tree branch or tangle of roots, a pale shadow scuttling at the edge of the visual field."[7]

Mary's preoccupation with the politically, historically, and, perhaps above all, gendered possibilities of communication, in the broadest sense of the word, was not just theoretical. Throughout her work, one also finds a sustained commitment to documenting the shifting possibilities and power granted to the teller of tales and, by extension, to the key question of what counts as a story or whose story is recognized as such and becomes authorized. In Mary's own formulation, *the social production of ephemerality* underwrites the iterative nonrecognition of women's contributions.[8] Produced as ephemeral, women's agency registers only as fleeting traces that skirt the contours of socially privileged stories or what, in a given place and time, counts as a story. Yet such traces gesture to other stories—"situated at the edge of exclusion"— that are easily overlooked and demand careful excavation.[9] Building on this attunement to detail and the telltale, Mary writes forensically for reconstruction and for pleasure, confronting complexity with careful, respectful engagement so as not to dissolve but rather to retain a sense of puzzlement.[10] All of this rests on a deep appreciation of the dense texture and mystery of even the most banal details of the everyday. Mary was especially sensitive to the uneventful regularity of daily life, to quotidian patterns and rhythms, to the expectations and imagination folded into them, and to the tenacity of the everyday even in the most unsettled of times. Such times included the hardship and deprivation associated with the struggle for independence in the Karo highlands.

Among the many engaging voices and personalities that populate Mary's writings are those of women who recalled for her in interviews the experience of shooting and eating an elephant during that period. Although Mary did not include this incident in *Rifle Reports*, she did make it the subject of a public talk that I heard at Harvard in April 2012. And, of course, she loved George Orwell's short essay from 1936 on "Shooting an Elephant."[11] The difference between the two is instructive. Orwell dwells on the psychological dilemma facing a young colonial officer, quietly if thoroughly disenchanted with the British Empire project, who recoils from the act of killing the great beast but knows he has no choice and, subsequently, mourns the animal's drawn out, tortured death that foreshadows India's violent partition and dismemberment some ten years later. Mary, by contrast, moves quickly past the shooting to home in on what mattered most to her informants: the serendipitous event of happening upon a potential meal in times of scarcity—not a good meal, mind you, but one that, under the circumstances, was good enough. From this, she draws out lessons regarding the relationships among memory, sensuous experience, community, and nation— importantly, from the perspective of postcolonial subjects looking back on events, from

---

[7] Mary Margaret Steedly, "Transparency and Apparition: Media Ghosts of Post-New Order Indonesia," in *Images That Move*, ed. Patricia Spyer and Mary Margaret Steedly (Sante Fe: School for Advanced Research Press, 2013), 281.

[8] Steedly, *Hanging without a Rope*, 29.

[9] Steedly, *Hanging without a Rope*, 31.

[10] Mary Margaret Steedly, "Eating an Elephant, Imagining a Community: Culinary Nationalism and the Memory of the Senses," elsewhere in this collection.

[11] George Orwell, "Shooting an Elephant," *New Writing* 2 (Autumn 1936).

big to deceivingly small—from the time of Indonesia's independence struggle on the northwestern fringe of the nation.

"Eating an elephant"—to be sure—is hardly an everyday occurrence in Karoland, today or in the past. But as Mary explains at the opening of her paper, the story provided the point of departure for conceptualizing what she admittedly "somewhat playfully" called culinary nationalism. Moreover, the essay offers a different spin on *Rifle Reports* and the many fresh provocations and conclusions it delivers in relation to central theoretical concepts and sociopolitical designations, such as the nation, experience, revolution, history, and modernity. Methodologically, "Eating an Elephant" exemplifies how Mary practiced the art of listening: as an embodied, sensuous activity. Consider, for instance, how Mary catches the resonance across Karoland, "on the outskirts of the nation," of *merdeka*, the Indonesian word for "freedom":

> What did they think they were taking part in [Mary asks rhetorically]? … For the most part, they had little sense either of "Indonesia" as a real or imagined entity, or even of "Karo" as an exclusive, perduring ethnic appellation. Freedom, as they imagined it, was "delicious" …
>
> "What's so funny?" I asked, poking my head in the doorway [this is Mary speaking] … "Listen to this" [answers one of Mary's assistants]. A girl's voice rolled tinnily from the tape recorder's small speakers: "So is that the only way to kill an elephant?" They [Mary's assistants] all shrieked with laughter again. [The hilarity was at the expense of a girl who spontaneously joined in the interview that Mary and a Karo relative, Ninin, conducted with Nande Wajib, who had worked as a nurse in a field hospital in the Karo highlands during the struggle for independence. The girl, perhaps a granddaughter, who Mary calls Sungkun Berita, was staying in the house at the time. Mary's assistants were reacting to the "random" character of the girl's questions and her insistence on pursuing her own concerns—in this case, "How does elephant meat taste?" And "which tastes better, elephant meat or beef?"]
>
> *Sungkun Berita:* How did they kill it?
>
> *Nande Wajib:* Shot it.
>
> *Sungkun Berita:* If it's shot is it sure to die?
>
> *Nande Wajib:* Yeah, if it's hit, you can kill it … They cut it up, divided the meat with local people …
>
> *Sungkun Berita:* Was the elephant meat tasty?
>
> *Nande Wajib:* Good enough, it was like beef.
>
> *Mary:* If you've been eating nothing but yams, well, it's tasty, right?
>
> *Nande Wajib:* It was good enough.
>
> *Sungkun Berita:* But now, compared to now, which tastes better, elephant meat or beef?
>
> *Nande Wajib:* Beef is better. How could an elephant be good to eat, because elephants work hard. Whenever they pass by, you know, *soouu* … that's the

sound they make. Not just one of them passes by. They travel in big groups. So if they go by, or if we know they want to go by, because their sound is really strong. So those people waited for them.

Sungkun Berita: So what do you do when they go by?

Nande Wajib: You hide! If they catch your scent, they'll chase you.

[A description follows about how elephants run—only in straight lines apparently—and how to avoid them—running in circles seems a good idea. Mary writes, "Near the interview's end, Sungkun Berita tried to recapture the frisson of dangerous encounters and strange foods by asking whether they had ever eaten snake meat."]

Nande Wajib: No, never. Why in the world would we eat snake? Oh, no!

I include this excerpt from Mary's elephant story to elaborate on some of the paper's themes, but also to draw out a few things that speak to who Mary was as a fieldworker, a collaborator, a Karo relative, a friend. Food is first and foremost among these. As she comes to the conclusion of her presentation, Mary observes, "I sometimes thought that a Karo history of the Independence struggle could be constructed entirely from stories about food, so frequently did they occur in our interviews … whenever food was mentioned you could be sure that you were being told something important."[12] Besides the importance of food there is pleasure—the pleasure Mary took in the company of the university students she hired to assist her in the transcription of taped interviews and in the other collaborations of her different research projects, in the sharing of stories, the serendipity of fieldwork, the idiosyncrasies and quirkiness of the people she met, and in the things they had to say to her and the stories they told. In the paper, her amusement at Nande Wajib's description of the elephant's habits and antics comes across, but so, too, does the pleasure she takes in the woman's dismissive response to the question as to whether she had ever eaten snake. When Mary presented the paper at Harvard, she had a hard time controlling her laughter at such moments.

I will end on a personal note. I also chose "telltale" as my keyword because it holds memories for me of Mary that are connected to our collaboration and long, close friendship. In the fall of 1983, before she left to begin fieldwork in North Sumatra, she visited me in Chicago where I was in graduate school. She brought me a remainder from cleaning out her Ann Arbor apartment, a wicker wastebasket that has stood under my desk ever since, in different parts of the world, and a gift, the book *Another Way of Telling*, by art historian John Berger and French photographer Jean Mohr, in which photographs of rural life in the French region of Savoye complement and contribute as much as the text.[13] Looking back, it seems propitious that the book comes out of a collaboration—indeed, one that combines images and text—and that its title resonates so clearly with the kind of focus Mary's fieldwork would take in Sumatra and that would be developed in *Hanging without a Rope*. In the book, I found an undated, handwritten letter wherein Mary writes about the trial of getting her research

---

[12] Steedly, "Eating an Elephant."

[13] John Berger and Jean Mohr, *Another Way of Telling: A Possible Theory of Photography* (New York: Pantheon Books, 1982).

visa for Indonesia (she blames the difficulty on Suharto's visit to the United States at the time) and a visit "down South" (where she was from):

> What else? The trip was uneventful, high point was dinner at the Mountain View Truck Stop in Tennessee, eating ham and turnip greens and cornbread and listening to the good ol' boys at the next table discuss the stock car races. So I'm back in the South and it feels good but God, Charlotte is boring. Suburbia for golden agers. Visited aunts and uncles, conversation turned on failure of uncles (75–85 years old) to pass driving tests.

Food, good Southern food and pleasure in the place, no doubt also the name of the place—the Mountain View Truck Stop—and in the conversation and ordinary fixtures of Southern life around her. Here is Mary also listening, always listening, taking everything in with her particular attunement to detail, her descriptive flair, and distinctive, somewhat wry sense of humor. As someone writing after Mary wrote and evoking a personal letter from her that I was delighted to find tucked between the pages of a book based on a close collaboration, I assume the role of the telltale in yet another sense—as one who betrays the confidence of another person, though not in a way I think Mary would have minded.

Last though not least, "telltale" also happens to be the name that Mary and I gave to what we envisioned as the second part of our multi-year collaborative project, "Signs of Crisis: Alternative Media and the Making of Political Identities in Southern Asia."[14] Conceived in the aftermath of the step-down in May 1998 of Indonesia's longtime authoritarian leader, Suharto, following months of student-led protest, we first spoke of a joint project when we shared a room at the annual meetings of the American Anthropological Association in the early 2000s, as we often did over the years. At the time, I was beginning to think about rumor, gossip, and hearsay; but also about graffiti, incendiary pamphlets, violent videos, and, somewhat later, huge Christian billboards and murals—the ephemeral mediations that made up what I described as an infrastructure of the imagination feeding into and co-producing, with other factors, the rampant uncertainty, violence, and terror of Ambon's religiously inflected war of the early 2000s.[15] At the time, Mary was working through the materials for her *Rifle Reports* book, but was also intrigued by the Indonesian craze for *horor* movies and television serials in the immediate post-Suharto years and what she came to understand as the fraught tension between a desire for transparency and revelation demanded by *Reformasi*, on the one hand, and the reticence and fear posed by anticipated openness and exposure, on the other.[16] As it turned out, we never made it past our initial focus on images. As the project progressed, we became increasingly engaged with questions of visuality, transparency, image circulation, affect, and publics or the kinds of issues we explored, with others, at a School of American Research advanced seminar that resulted in the coedited volume *Images That Move*. As

---

[14] This Harvard-Leiden research program was funded by the Harvard Peabody Museum and the Netherlands Organization for Scientific Research (NWO) Humanities Division.

[15] Patricia Spyer, *Orphaned Landscapes: Violence, Visuality, and the Work of Appearances in Post-Authoritarian Indonesia* (New York: Fordham University Press, under advance contract); and "Fire without Smoke and Other Phantoms of Ambon's Violence: Media Effects, Agency, and the Work of Imagination," *Indonesia* 74 (2002): 1–16.

[16] Steedly, "Transparency and Apparition."

so often happens, we got caught up in the work on that and our money ran out in the meantime (as it often does). But I also recognize, with immense regret, that if Mary had had more time, we might have very well picked up telltale again like the axe in Pak Tua's story or, more likely, come up with something new that we wanted to share and work on together.

GENDER

Carla Jones

Even when gender was not at the center of Mary's analytical frame, it was. In revisiting her work now, I find myself returning to a current concept: intersectionality. Mary's analyses were intersectional before we thought of them that way and even when her informants did not consider gender at the core of their own stories. Mary saw a world of intersecting lives, forces, and things. Hers was a world of relationships.[1]

Never a single thing, gender was always a point of view. This is most evident in her concept of "the social production of ephemerality," in which the feminine was consistently, but not inevitably, pushed to the edges of respected life.[2] This ephemerality was marginalizing, devaluing, and in some respects impossible to escape. Yet Mary never stopped there. She gave us the joy, pride, and accomplishment her subjects also experienced, by way of theorizing experience itself. By studying the edges of life, the excess that social disorder produced, she argued that we could more clearly see the partiality that undergirds the illusion of order emanating from stories told by those at the center of the action. Put differently, although there was hierarchy and violence in Mary's world, there was also dependence.

By visiting a world where subjects were perpetually at risk of exceeding boundaries of propriety, where spirits and people merged, where people, things, or animals needed each other, Mary also captured an important fact: that we are always touching each other, that we are split, relational selves that cannot exist without others.

Carla Jones is an associate professor in the anthropology department at the University of Colorado–Boulder.

[1] I use the concept of intersectionality slightly differently here than its original meaning in feminist legal theory. Rather than refer to the ways that intersecting subject positions can amplify structural marginalization, I suggest that Mary's analytic and personal perspective allowed her to see intersections across a diverse range of relationships with humans and nonhumans.

[2] Mary Margaret Steedly, *Hanging without a Rope: Narrative Experience in Colonial and Postcolonial Karoland* (Princeton: Princeton University Press, 1993), 29.

This has been a core concept in feminist theory, yet Mary found a way to convey that fact through refusing the binary nature often ascribed to gender. So many of the topics she studied already had established, conventional accounts of cause and effect. Colonialism begets nationalism. War begets trauma. Mary rejected these categories, much as she rejected a simple account of men oppressing women. Yet this did not mean she ignored ideology or the violence of a dominant narrative. For example, as she showed, women and men were summoned to different roles during the Indonesian revolution, and their accounts afterward were perhaps unsurprisingly different.

Female recruits in the revolutionary army in the Dutch East Indies of 1945–49 entered into a kind of social and political chaos, freed from some of the norms of domesticity, able to move across the landscape, able to wear different clothes, able to violate some (but not all) social norms because the world was fleetingly upside down. Mary aptly described this as "eagerness," a particular translation of the Malay term *meliar* that underscored its ambiguity. Eager girls were a combination of industry and wildness, perpetually on the verge of "enthusiastic participation and promiscuous disorder."[3]

The official account of Indonesian nationalism is a story of twinned independences in which collective, national independence would be realized through a heroic, masculine model of personal independence. Mary's accounts of female veterans added their brief, thrilling sojourns into freedom to that account. Their experience of *zaman merdeka* was the best time of their lives, almost a kind of paradise.[4] As proof of that inverted world, parents sent their daughters to war to protect them, rather than the reverse. Proper members of the Srikandi Corps were trained to march in formation, wear simple uniforms, and fire weapons, as well as cook and clean for the real (male) soldiers. As one village headman said to Mary, women cooked before, during, and after the war, so they could not have struggled much during the revolution itself.[5] Mary's elicitation of stories of the banality of war showed how wrong that was. These stories gave us the glamour, routine, and exhaustion women veterans recalled. If in war women were at once different from men and not, then could they also be heroes?

In revisiting this question, I return to the versions of the past in Karo Batak histories Mary offers us, and also recall her more recent work on female cadets at the Citadel in Charleston, SC. In each case, women could not win for trying. They were either blamed for attempting to be too masculine and denying their feminine natures, or dismissed for being too feminine to ever compete in a man's world. While Mary kept this frustrating, persistent fact in sight, it was the examples of women and men who denied these rigid categories that were most interesting, that motivated her to keep thinking, and to refuse a world in which we are not all interconnected and where women's contributions are not acknowledged. Only Mary's detailed, careful research into women's memories could offer alternative versions of the past, one in which chaos revealed networks of *dependence*, mutuality, and even altruism. Those connections were not simply among humans, but among humans and spirits, humans and objects, and

---

[3] Mary Margaret Steedly, *Rifle Reports: A Story of Indonesian Independence* (Berkeley: University of California Press, 2013), 207.

[4] Steedly, *Rifle Reports*, 52.

[5] Steedly, *Rifle Reports*, 49.

humans and animals. Nandé Laga, the captivating trader, healer, and spirit medium at the core of *Hanging without a Rope*, could not revisit the past without her magic staff. Indonesian war veteran Cik Muham felt that firing a rifle was essential to her revolutionary role. Suzzanna, the Indonesian horror film queen beloved by Indonesians and Mary alike, could not channel spirits without serpents.[6] Raja Bakaléwat, protagonist of Batak myths, could not have survived his adventure without his dog.[7] Despite Mary's being an intensely private person, her work nevertheless reveals a world saturated with intimate connections. She saw ties others did not.

The accounts she shared involve delight, but also anger. Interestingly, these feelings seemed most apparent when spirits expressed them. By definition ephemeral, spirits chose to speak in women's voices in part to gain access to the human world, but also chose to do so through people who were similarly ephemeral. Mary insisted that it was never clear who was speaking "through whom." Whose identity preceded the utterance? And who could understand it? Karo men heard one thing while Karo women heard another. Nandé Laga's dilemma, and therefore our own, was thus to realize that "one may speak for oneself and not be understood, or speak as someone else and convene an audience."[8] Mary's precise, lyrical writing captured this conundrum elegantly, because in revisiting Nandé Laga's utterances now one must still delight in her dancing.

Mary's later work on haunting and horror insisted on the same insight. Could Indonesian horror films exist without the tantalizing fusion of sexuality and visuality? It was as if the most powerful way to convey the power of secrecy was through an image of a woman in a bikini, and in the world's largest majority Muslim country during a time in which women's dress had become increasingly covered. Because the angriest spirits in these films were female, harnessing their stories to contemporary gendered violence, like the plight of migrant workers or the victims of sexual assault during the anti-Soeharto protests in 1998, was almost readymade. Indeed, Indonesian activists did exactly that.

Mary loved to remind us that horror's power rested in not showing. The bits we could only imagine were more powerful than the truth itself. Illusion and allusion worked together, yet still never explained everything. Across diverse research settings from North Carolina to Sumatra, Jakarta, and then South Carolina, I now sense her insistence on the pairs of seeing and belief, evidence and faith, and collective and personal disorder. As Pastor Vernon Cooper, the Lumbee healer in North Carolina who was at the center of her 1979 master's thesis in folklore, said to her about the challenge of healing invisible ailments, "You've got to reach out where there's nothing and grab something."[9] Mary seemed to take his advice in the decades that followed, "reaching out" herself by always being willing to accept that the world is more than it

---

[6] Mary Margaret Steedly, "Transparency and Apparition: Media Ghosts of Post-New Order Indonesia," in *Images That Move*, ed. Patricia Spyer and Mary Margaret Steedly (Santa Fe: School for Advanced Research Press, 2013).

[7] Mary Margaret Steedly, "Surrogates, Slips, and Incidental Intrusions: The Tale of Raja Bakaléwat's Dog," *Anthropology and Humanism* 24, 2 (1999): 109–16.

[8] Steedly, *Hanging without a Rope*, 198.

[9] Mary Margaret Steedly, "The Evidence of Things Not Seen: Faith and Tradition in a Lumbee Healing Practice" (master's thesis, Curriculum in Folklore, University of North Carolina—Chapel Hill, 1979), 104.

seems. For people whose visible performances are especially subject to public scrutiny—women—the power to use visible declarations, through dress or claims to national revolutionary respect, still bumped up against the unspoken assumptions that women were ephemeral precisely because of their belief in surfaces. Mary never let go of the perception that social disorder affects personal life, for good or for ill. While her thesis respectfully conveyed Pastor Cooper's observation that the illnesses he treated were an effect of the broader dislocation and marginalization of Lumbee subjects in North Carolina, the social disorder that characterized "independence times" in Sumatra allowed at least some Karo Batak women to relish a little risk. It was as if she continued to channel Pastor Cooper's observation that "feeling is the door to understanding."[10]

The voices that were most interesting to Mary had the habit of appearing in times of crisis: communal, national, or epic. She never let us think that these voices were single, just as the selves she focused on never were, either. Contrary to Western psychological theory that presupposes a discrete, integrated self, Mary's world was populated with people who were healthier for their partiality and mutuality. Piah Manik, wife of the renowned revolutionary hero Selamat Ginting, insisted she was simply a "faithful companion" rather than a hero herself.[11] Rather than selves needing to be revealed, these were selves that were experienced and made through their bonds to others.

Mary's research and professional styles were as eager as those of the girls she studied: conducting fieldwork in remote, but not isolated, areas that could only be accessed by motorbike or foot; denying herself sleep to stay up through the night to find a particular *warung*, or to hang with out with friends and fellow researchers; and enduring Jakarta traffic when she would have preferred the mountains. These adventures seemed to offer Mary her own paradise. There was always another delicious dish or another version of a story to savor along the way.

Multiple generations of young scholars, especially those who work in Southeast Asia, benefited from Mary's enthusiasm for mutual interests. The careerist description of her generosity might be to say that she shared her networks. Another would be to simply recognize that she enacted her worldview of mutual dependence through forthright, frank yet supportive feedback. She was exceptional for generously introducing doctoral students to senior scholars, praising everyone along the way. There was room in the conversation for everyone in her world. My own favorite memories of her are of spontaneous multi-hour conversations in hotel hallways during professional conferences. Meandering, intense, brilliant, I now wish I had recorded them. This quality informed one of her widely known yet undervalued talents as a panel discussant. A good discussant is part cheerleader and part critic, kindly connecting disparate threads into, if not a coherent story, then at least a series of new questions. Mary seemed to have infinite energy for seeing the central point of a paper that the author themself had missed, to weave that into a concept by a fellow presenter, and to then ask how these details might expand or redirect a particular theoretical debate in the discipline. Never stingy, Mary posed sharp questions that

---

[10] Steedly, "The Evidence of Things Not Seen," 121.
[11] Steedly, "The Evidence of Things Not Seen," 90.

were obvious only when she posed them. In an academic economy in which ideas are currency, she offered hers as gifts without expectation of reciprocity. What could be a more fundamentally feminist act?

Mary's own theoretical contributions put her in the league of Indonesianist scholars whose analyses have contributed to the discipline more broadly. Indonesia enjoys a unique role in American anthropology as a generative site for cultural theory. The reasons for this influence are likely varied, including the close resonance among the variety of cultural forms across the archipelago with shifting theoretical trends like modernization, structuralism, or interpretive anthropology. These insights sometimes contributed to a problematic category called "culture," which Mary found too broad to usefully describe the lives of people she knew. Like culture, gender could also be an instrument of "dangerous utility," even as smaller identitarian classifications risked reproducing the problems they were meant to solve.[12] Notably, the first keyword listed in her 1999 *Annual Review of Anthropology* article on culture theory was neither culture nor theory, but gender. "Writing around" gender offered new potential.[13] It could shift our gaze away from explanation and toward empathy and complexity. Analyses of institutional forms of gendered identity, for example, could thus be useful in recognizing how states, or nationalisms, or "cultures" enact their capacity to create a patina of uniformity or elide dissent. In other words, without intending it, writing around gender could lead to places we never expect, from the grim study of violence to the pleasures of watching horror films. It might even lead us back to culture, which "might now be worth another look."[14]

It feels too soon to be saying this, but in a moment in the United States in which public nationalism seems to have taken a single, masculine form, we benefit from remembering Mary's insight that crises can animate divergent, feminine forms of national community. I wonder what details she might see were she with us still. She might invite us to seek contemporary equivalents to Nandé Laga, Piah Manik, or even Suzanna. She might suggest that we empathetically expand our analytic frame beyond the obvious heroes to include the unspoken, the unseen, or simply the disdained. She might notice the totemic objects enhancing the potency of political life, and the ways those objects might be repurposed to oppositional ends, yet still misrecognized. She might see eagerness where others see exhaustion. She might even remind us that chaos can produce the best time of our lives.

For this, and many more reasons, we have deep cause to miss her. I miss her.

---

[12] Mary Margaret Steedly, "What Is Culture? Does It Matter?" in *Field Work: Sites in Literary and Cultural Studies*, ed. Marjorie Garber, Paul B. Franklin, and Rebecca L. Walkowitz (New York: Routledge, 1996), 23.

[13] Steedly, "What Is Culture? Does It Matter?" 23.

[14] Mary Margaret Steedly, "The State of Culture Theory in the Anthropology of Southeast Asia," *Annual Review of Anthropology* 28 (1999): 446.

CULTURE

Smita Lahiri

> Quite simply, "culture" makes me uncomfortable.
> —Mary M. Steedly

A mistress of the title phrase, Mary knew how to crisply delineate her subject matter while evoking a train of resonant associations. Her knack for turning a phrase showed in the distinctive names she gave many of her courses and research projects, including "Colonial Departures," "After Images," and "Other Others." But once during my time in the Harvard anthropology department, she unveiled a new graduate seminar whose name seemed uncharacteristically flat. Lacking even the usual colon and elaborating phrase, it was simply entitled "Culture."

In due time, a poster advertising the course to students went up on the walls of William James Hall. It featured an iconic photo of Franz Boas taken ca. 1895 in the Smithsonian Museum, where Boas was at the time employed. With the avid beam of a conjuror, the father of American anthropology squatted with a hoop in both hands, recreating a Hamat'sa dance from memory as he staged a forthcoming gallery exhibit. To present-day eyes, he cut a Chaplinesque figure: dated, risible, yet irresistible all at once. Looking as if he might leap off the course flyer at any moment, Boas seemed to be winking at the bolded word "Culture," as if somehow conspiring in league with Mary. But for what ends?

The following spring, Mary decided to rebrand her "Culture" course as the second half of the graduate proseminar and invited me to co-teach it with her. Mary had already been my role model and mentor in the department, and the invitation, which came just as we were also becoming friends, was one of her most precious gifts to me. For one thing, it taught me that the co-taught classroom can be a gloriously freeing space. I found it far easier to loosen up and riff on ideas while Mary was generously shepherding the discussion and keeping an eye on the time. Although we were never

---

Smita Lahiri is a lecturer in anthropology and international affairs at the University of New Hampshire.

really sure how the first-year students were feeling about it all, I'd like to think that co-teaching was as pleasurable for Mary as it was for me.

Mary's post-traditional approach to culture theory was probably as foundational for me as it was for any of our students. Her take on things was unjaded, unapologetic, and critical; her approach, both forensic and intuitive. She often read key passages out loud, particularly during the early weeks of the course, while we were retracing the emergence and establishment of a distinctively American tradition of cultural anthropology. When Mary uncorked works by Boas, Mead, and Hurston, a redolence of the early twentieth-century Upper West Side came wafting in, accented by hints of *eau de* Sepik, Eatonville, and Baffin Island.[1] To switch sensory registers, Mary made anthropology's ancestral voices resound in our ears. She asked us to hear the spaces between the notes, the silences in the texts.

As this essay's epigraph indicates, "culture" made Mary uncomfortable.[2] This is not too surprising, considering that her generation of anthropologists was the first to recognize the concept's many flaws, along with its weaponization within colonial and postcolonial power relations. But Mary's stance becomes more intriguing when conjoined with how deeply she continued to think about "culture" long after so many formidable intellects—her peers—had discarded it.

Why, in 2010, had Mary decided to offer a course on culture theory? She certainly wasn't channeling old-school nostalgia, taking a crack at a dead horse, or hatching a practical joke on bemused graduate students. While I cannot answer the question for her, I will try to address it on the basis of what Mary wrote and said, not only in the classroom but in our many conversations "around" the subject of culture. In particular, I want to explore how she sat with her discomfort, eventually finding ways of attending to the problematic and politicized weight of "culture" even as she built on those features of traditional ethnography that remained compelling to her.

In "What is Culture?" Mary touches on her master's thesis, which emerged from her first fieldwork experience in Robeson County, North Carolina.[3] A portrayal of a Lumbee curer named Vernon Cooper, the thesis displayed the eloquence that would mark her later writing, but it was also a product of its time. This much is clear from Mary's rather structuralist analysis, which attributes Cooper's efficacy as a curer to his success in mapping individual illnesses upon the larger malaise of the Lumbee social body.

After a gap of some years, Mary reflected on how she felt about this argument:

> I hated it so much that I never gave Mr. Cooper a copy of my thesis, even though there was nothing in it that I thought (or still think) was not actually respectful of him ... something about the writing of it bothered me immensely.

---

[1] The texts assigned for the course included Franz Boas, "A Year among the Eskimo," *Journal of the American Geographical Society of New York* 19 (1887): 383–402, as well as selections from Margaret Mead, *Sex and Temperament in Three Primitive Societies* (Oxford: William Morrow, 1935), and Zora Neale Hurston, *Mules and Men* (Philadelphia: J. B. Lippincott Co., 1935).

[2] Mary Margaret Steedly, "What is Culture? Does it Matter?" in *Field Work: Sites In Literary and Cultural Studies*, ed. Marjorie Garber, Paul B. Franklin, and Rebecca L. Walkowitz (New York: Routledge, 1996), 19.

[3] See James Peacock's contribution elsewhere in this issue.

It seemed that turning people or events or texts or stories into illustrations, prototypes, or "sites" of something else erased the very thing that I wanted to capture in writing about them in the first place ... Lumbee "culture" did not explain Mr. Cooper's curing practice, and his curing activities were not just an illustration of some general cultural principle. Using them in this way felt rather like a betrayal.[4]

Mary's guilty sense of having done Cooper a disservice had enduring consequences. For out of it emerged a unique style of ethnographic representation, one that was grounded in the dialogical nature of stories and attuned to social practices of re-voicing narrated experience. In a sense, stories gave Mary the means to implement Vernon Cooper's first principle for dealing with unseen forces: "you've got to reach out where there's nothing and grab something."[5]

This may be easier to follow if one understands that Mary regarded stories as belonging to two notionally distinct but thoroughly entwined orders of reality: experience and memory. Since primary experience is always at the point of vanishing, even for its subjects, it is only and inevitably through personal (and, in different ways, collective) memory that it can become publicly expressed and accessed anew. The two orders of reality coming together in narrative, for the act of recollection before an audience, whether real or fantasized, constitutes its own form of experience. This, in a roundabout way, brought Mary back to "culture." Stories became a privileged point of entry into culture as a manifold of potential significations that each storyteller actualizes in his or her own particular, partial, and socially influenced way. Not surprisingly, then, Mary's signature way of writing ethnography (one could say, of writing culture) was to retell someone else's story for purposes of her own. And while her topics and concerns ranged widely, they inevitably included the textuality of the story itself: how it had been told, what had occasioned its telling, and how it had fared with its audience, whether proximate or far-removed.

Mary's first book, *Hanging without a Rope,* interleaves texts, settings, and voices to stunning effect, all the while advancing important conversations about gender, power, marginality, and regional scholarship on "Karoland," i.e., North Sumatra.[6] As Karen Strassler says, it is a book that gets inside the reader.[7] But perhaps because it is an infuriatingly difficult book to summarize, its uptake and influence have been diffuse. The scope of *Rifle Reports,* her second book and *magnum opus* on the Indonesian Revolution, is more easily grasped, since it is bounded by the years 1945–49, when, following the end of the Japanese Occupation, forces bent on Dutch reoccupation were beaten back by local, loosely coordinated militias all across present-day Indonesia.[8]

---

[4] Steedly, "What is Culture?" 20.

[5] From Mary's master's thesis, quoted in Carla Jones's essay elsewhere in this collection. My thanks to Carla Jones for sharing Mary's master's thesis with me.

[6] Mary Margaret Steedly, *Hanging without a Rope: Narrative Experience in Colonial and Postcolonial Karoland* (Princeton: Princeton University Press, 1993).

[7] See Karen Strassler's contribution, "Memory," elsewhere in this issue, in which she recalls that "Mary's book worked on me."

[8] Mary Margaret Steedly, *Rifle Reports: A Story of Indonesian Independence* (Berkeley: University of California Press, 2013).

Mary based *Rifle Reports* on myriad published sources and on long-term fieldwork during the 1990s, when she sought out elderly men and women who recalled the mass upheavals in Karoland during this short but momentous period. Despite its seemingly tight focus, the book's scope widens ever further as it discloses the inscription of experience in official history, personal memory, and the senses. It delineates what was valorized and what was set aside, explores elisions at the edge of conventional narratives of the revolution, and locates fugitive, often gendered elements that slipped through these conventions to lodge in the realms of the sensory and quotidian.

In *Hanging without a Rope,* Mary had explored women's subalternity through narrative, asking why women's personal stories were rarely credited with coherence and authority in comparison with those told by men. In writing *Rifle Reports,* she found this phenomenon magnified, since women's roles in fighting the Dutch—the paradigmatic activity of *revolusi*—were at best auxiliary, and also because after independence demobilized women were recruited to embody properly national roles as wives and mothers in a cult of domesticity that one critic later dubbed "State Ibuism."[9] Those who supported the fighters, survived, fled the fighting, or otherwise had their lives disrupted during the resistance found few opportunities to speak of their struggles once these were over.

Mary was thus venturing into uncharted territory, but so, too, were the women who shared their motley recollections of using red dishcloths as signals, living by their wits, or evacuating with children to a strange landscape. That their experiences deserved to be recognized was clear, but (possibly informed by the shadow of Vernon Cooper) what Mary assembled from these bits and pieces was no straightforward account of unsung heroism. Instead, she chose to honor their fragmentary quality as subaltern narratives together with the complexities of voicing, the occasions of telling, and the purposes of storytellers. Mary also veered subtly off the anthropologist's traditional path of cultural translation toward what might be more aptly called "cultural transcreation." Situating each story afresh, putting it in conversation with other sources of information—songs, genealogies, official records, authoritative accounts—she sought to open up an entire horizon of refracted significances before a new audience.

Several of these strategies come into play in the second chapter of *Rifle Reports,* "Buried Guns," where Mary weaves a tapestry of Karo revolutionary turbulence around the apparently still figure of Piah Manik.[10] As the sheltered daughter of one militia man and the young wife of another, Piah Manik's role in their exploits during 1945–49 was as quotidian and circumscribed as was the life she subsequently led as the wife of a lionized freedom fighter and local politician. Her husband, Selamat Ginting, was best known for an act of bravura that marked a turning point in national and regional history. Sukarno and Hatta declared Indonesian independence from Java immediately after the Japanese surrender in August 1949. Two months passed, yet the revolutionary brass in Medan still hemmed and hawed, fearful of raising the flag lest their military capacity prove insufficient in the event of a retaliatory Dutch surge. Into

---

[9] Julia Suryakusuma, "The State and Sexuality in New Order Indonesia," in *Fantasizing the Feminine in Indonesia,* ed. Laurie J. Sears (Durham: Duke University Press), 92–119.

[10] Steedly, *Rifle Reports,* 71–112.

this impasse stepped the swashbuckling Selamat Ginting. In what amounted to a rebuke as well as a challenge, he produced a hidden cache of Japanese arms and delivered these weapons to the leaders in Medan. Duly galvanized, they declared Indonesian independence and the revolution in Sumatra was officially launched.

"Buried Guns" adopts Piah Manik's point of view in narrating what led up to this heralded moment. The chapter opens with an account of Selamat Ginting's funeral in 1994, which Mary attended shortly after arranging to interview the ailing hero about women's roles in the North Sumatran resistance. A mournful Piah Manik offered to make good on her husband's promise, warning that whatever she had to say would be a poor substitute for the authoritative account that the man she called "Bapak" ("father," also an honorific for national heroes) would have provided. Sure enough, when next they met, Piah Manik recounted her life as a series of footnotes to her husband's exploits, a string of acts of "domestic industry" carried out while following her husband from place to place in flight from the Dutch. At one point, the flatness of her chronicle prompts Mary to ask, "How do you recognize the subject in the story of a faithful companion?"[11]

One of Mary's strategies in meeting this challenge was to play off text against context. Thus, "Buried Guns" honors the "affective core"[12] of wifely loyalty at the heart of Piah Manik's story, even as it reveals the centrality of Piah Manik's social networks in enabling Selamat Ginting to acquire the guns from a sympathetic Occupation official and of women's wartime activities of production and provisioning. Another strategy Mary used was to exploit the intrinsically refractory quality of narrative discourse. For example, "Buried Guns" finds its unhurried way into an inadvertent "loophole"[13] in Piah Manik's meandering story about the part she played in burying the famous guns in a rice field. In spite of herself, the comedy of errors she relates does less to substantiate Selamat Ginting's glorious reputation than to render him faintly ridiculous.

Since the highly born Bapak did not know his way to the logical hiding place in his family's upland fields, it fell to Piah Manik to bury them there. The cache of guns was a large one, so Piah Manik mustered a work party for the feigned reason of transporting sacks of rice bran to the family's furthest dry field to scatter for pest control. She packed each sack with guns, hiding their contents from her helpers by placing them between layers of old clothes and topping them off with a layer of rice bran. Once the guns had reached the field, she sent her helpers home on some pretext even as Bapak stole out to rendezvous with her. Even now, things did not run smoothly, for just as the couple was getting ready to dig a servant unexpectedly showed up, sending Bapak into a funk. Only after Piah helped dispatch the servant with another ruse (this time a ribald one) did they get down to it. But since Bapak wasn't much good with the hoe

---

[11] Steedly, *Rifle Reports*, 89. Here Mary references one of the seminal works of subaltern historiography. See Gayatri Chakraborty Spivak, "Can the Subaltern Speak?" in *Colonial Discourse and Postcolonial Theory: A Reader*, ed. Patrick Williams and Laura Chrisman (New York: Columbia University Press, 1994), 66–11.

[12] Steedly, *Rifle Reports*, 69.

[13] As Mary explained in *Hanging without a Rope* (200), the Bakhtinian concept of "loophole" refers to an effect of reported speech wherein a speaker subverts another's message merely (and hence blamelessly) by voicing their discourse from a different social location.

and she'd had plenty of practice growing dry rice for the household during those lean times, it was Piah Manik who did most of the digging.

In "Buried Guns," Mary peels back the legend of how Selamat Ginting made history in Medan to reveal an understory centered upon the figure of a resourceful and competent backcountry woman. In "transcreating" Piah's account, Mary included details that might have dropped out of a more conventional treatment of women's revolutionary participation. As always, she knew just what she was doing:

> I have opted for a narrative style built upon apparent digressions, an accumulation of discursive layers, careful attention to detail and texture, shifting temporalities, and self-conscious interventions. My intention is to produce an account that moves towards difficulty rather than simplification, one that compels as well as enacts the strategies of patient reading, aiming not to get to the bottom of things but rather to sink […] ever deeper into the intense narrativity of everyday life … [14]

Unpracticed at telling her story, Piah Manik found her memory failing her at certain points, while at others she went off on tangents about the tricky business of dry rice farming. But each of these interruptions tells us something about the ways in which women soldiered through the revolution by doing what needed to be done, making their lives "narratable" and "remarkable"[15] even if nobody paid much attention afterward. Indeed, Mary's entire body of work was informed by the idea that hegemonic articulations of culture smooth out much of the nubbiness of social reality. It was also buoyed by her love of listening to people and her understanding that the everyday transmission of culture is necessarily entangled with narrative and is therefore vulnerable to it. And so there will always be stray storylines, loose threads that will unravel the tight fabric of "culture" if we can only tug on them in the right way.

Almost a decade after Mary invited me to co-teach it with her, I'm still learning from her "Culture" course. I believe that one reason Mary kept reading Boas and the Boasians was her intuition that, behind all the dreary talk of "the superorganic" and "the arc of human potential," figures like Kroeber and Mead had been moved, like herself, by witnessing an entire horizon of cultural signification refracted in a particular person's lives and words. As did so many others, Mary dealt with the intellectual tumult of the 1970s and 1980s by breaking the sacred mold of "culture" bequeathed by disciplinary forbears. Unlike many of her contemporaries, however, she never threw away the pieces.

---

[14] Steedly, *Rifle Reports*, 69.
[15] Steedly, *Rifle Reports*, 112.

AUDIENCE

Ann Marie Leshkowich

Mary Steedly was a consummate storyteller. What made her so was not her mastery of cadence, word choice, and the twists and turns of daily experience. Nor was it her delight in the unexpected, the incongruous, and the ineffable. Of course, Mary excelled at all of these elements of the art, but her virtuosity lay in her knowledge of how to audience.

What does it mean "to audience"? I use a verb form deliberately to capture what Mary in *Hanging without a Rope* analyzed as audiencing practice. In her first book, Mary considers how women's voices are marginalized. This marginalization occurs not simply in the sense of women not being able to speak, although gender-based silencing occurs with frequency and ferocity. But it also involves what happens when women do voice their perspectives. Who listens and hears? Whose voices matter? Typically not those of women, for, as Mary observes, "the language of subjects and objects" is one in which "women, being neither, are continually left out of the count."[1]

In her essay in the influential edited volume *Power and Difference*, Anna Tsing notes that "'power means…the ability to convene an audience.'"[2] Mary elaborates upon this point:

> This is not, of course, simply a matter of drawing a crowd, but rather of gaining attentive and comprehending listeners, which requires narrative plausibility as much as strategic self-dramatization. Convening an audience means telling the kind of story that counts for something to those for whom it is intended. It is in

---

Ann Marie Leshkowich is a professor of anthropology at College of the Holy Cross, Worcester, Massachusetts.

[1] Mary Margaret Steedly, *Hanging without a Rope: Narrative Experience in Colonial and Postcolonial Karoland* (Princeton: Princeton University Press, 1993), 198.

[2] Anna Lowenhaupt Tsing, "Gender and Performance in Meratus Dispute Settlement," in *Power and Difference: Gender in Island Southeast Asia*, ed. Jane Monnig Atkinson and Shelly Errington (Stanford: Stanford University Press, 1990), 122; quoted in Steedly, *Hanging without a Rope*, 198.

this dialogue of plausible voices and convened audiences that narrative experience, ours and others', is constituted.[3]

Women in Karoland, Mary tells us, can, on the one hand, speak and not be understood. On the other hand, they can "speak as someone else and convene an audience."[4] The problem has not been that women have not spoken. Rather, it is that they have not had audiences for what they might be saying when they speak as themselves.

Having made a point about the gendered politics of voicing and audiencing in Karoland, Mary, in a characteristic move, shifts the reader's focus from ethnographic terrain to a meditation on the power relationship embedded in writing and reading anthropological texts. Addressing her readers—an audience that she has convened through her act of authorship—as fellow anthropologists and humans inhabiting social worlds rich with meaning, Mary offers a two-part charge so that we readers might learn how to audience. First, we need to look for stories that do not follow the script, ones that she describes as "persistently 'elsewhere' in our grids and codes."[5] Such stories are not neat. They do not offer consistency and closure. They do not deliver a lesson or moral, but their very messiness, their uncorralled excess, carries potent possibilities.[6]

Mary's second challenge to her audience is to attend to the interactive sociality of narration by recognizing ourselves as both speakers and listeners. As Mary asks, "To whom do we, as storytellers, speak? How do we go about constructing a story compelling to that audience? Or, to put it differently, how do we convince our audiences that our stories are compelling?"[7] Stories are shaped by their audiences. We, as anthropologists, as scholars, as co-humans, and as companion species, are not just tellers of stories, our own and those of others. We are the hearers of those stories, and it is in our listening that the worldmaking potential of stories can flourish. In Mary's words, we—especially scholars, who tend to prize our ability to give voice to our views—"need to learn to convene ourselves as someone else's audience, to learn to listen to someone else speaking."[8] Mary's next sentence, my favorite from all of her work, echoes often in my mind as I listen and speak: "And we need to find ways of shaping our stories less to

---

[3] Steedly, *Hanging without a Rope*, 198.

[4] Steedly, *Hanging without a Rope*, 198.

[5] Steedly, *Hanging without a Rope*, 199.

[6] Mary was one of many groundbreaking feminist scholars in the 1980s and 1990s to explore connections among storytelling, gender, identity, and power. Let me give just two other examples, both from scholars whose work came to my attention through Mary's teaching and who, along with Mary, have subsequently shaped much of my thinking about narrative, gender, and subjectivity. In *Woman, Native, Other*, Trinh T. Minh-ha argues that the dominance of narrative conventions associated with formal history dismisses the stories told by women and others who have been marginalized—and with them the connections, the identities, the feelings, and knowledge that those stories multi-sensorily permit and transmit (Trinh T. Minh-ha, *Woman, Native, Other: Writing Postcoloniality and Feminism* [Bloomington: Indiana University Press, 1989]). Focusing on the intersections between gender and class, Carolyn Kay Steedman's *Landscape for a Good Woman* draws our attention to "lives lived out on the borderlands, lives for which the central interpretative devices of the culture don't quite work" (Carolyn Kay Steedman, *Landscape for a Good Woman: A Story of Two Lives* [New Brunswick: Rutgers University Press, 1986], 5).

[7] Steedly, *Hanging without a Rope*, 199.

[8] Steedly, *Hanging without a Rope*, 199.

the plausible demands of the ready-made grid and the fully elaborated code and more to the everyday cadences of the perpetual open end."⁹

Mary further urges us to recognize that the speaking subject is neither discrete nor fully responsible for the comprehensibility of that which is said. Words in speech are mine and not mine, yours and not yours. They are evocatively suspended, bloated with intentions. Voices, too, are heterogeneous, heterodox, fragmentary, and multiple. "As mediums recognize," Mary writes, "voices are never singular, meaning is always negotiated, and there is room enough in any story for someone else's speaking."¹⁰

I'm going to tell you a story. Because I lack Mary's narrative gifts, I will tell it clumsily. I'll tell it self-consciously, because it involves me, and I am not good at talking about myself. I will tell it in a rather linear fashion, because that is my way. No matter how much I try, the everyday cadences of the perpetual open end are not where I feel most at home. I'll tell the story to you, the audience convened through this journal, and it will be ours, even as it is also not ours. Some of you will have heard some of the story before—more on that in a moment.

The story is about a ceramic bunny in a field in southern Vietnam. During my dissertation fieldwork in the mid-1990s, Mary announced that she wanted to visit me in Ho Chi Minh City on her way back from Indonesia, where she had been completing interviews for Rifle Reports. *She stayed with me for a few days. I tried to show her around. A friend with a private car, something unusual in Vietnam at that time, took us to several sites in the provinces surrounding the city. On the way back, the highway passed through an area known for its ceramic factories. There, in a field, hundreds of ceramic bunnies sat erect, perched at attention.*

We stopped and got out of the car. Mary and I were both enraptured by the bunnies' winsome expressions [Figure 1]. *Clearly mass produced, each bunny nonetheless had individual facial quirks and slightly jaunty bodily positions, as if they had been frozen in mid-twitch. Mind you, these were not bunnies for sale, at least not at that particular moment. They had been produced in large quantities and were likely waiting to be packed into a container and shipped somewhere.*

Mary and I immediately decided that we each needed to have one. In the midst of the rapid changes that Vietnam was experiencing, that bunny had a story to tell. Indeed, it pointed to a sense of possibility, that open-ended cadence in the midst of industrial uniformity. We picked up two bunnies, went in search of the facility's management office, and negotiated a price with a

---

⁹ Steedly, *Hanging without a Rope*, 199.

¹⁰ Steedly, *Hanging without a Rope*, 201. "Audiencing" would similarly be a central concern of Mary's second monograph. Alongside "stories of Indonesian independence that could be told from the outskirts of the nation," *Rifle Reports* explores "the work of storytelling both as memory practice and as ethnographic genre: how stories of personal experience are told and received; how past events are recalled and reworked in storied form; how narrative plausibility is constructed or dismantled; how the art of narration constitutes its subject(s)—in short, how stories inhabit social space and sociability abides in stories"; see Mary Margaret Steedly, *Rifle Reports: A Story of Indonesian Independence* (Berkeley: University of California Press, 2013), 9. Mary again reminds her audience/readership that ethnographers engage in audiencing practice; the sympathy we often feel with those whose stories we hear forges additional links in the chains of narrative seduction that we need to attend to as matters of genre and performativity (ibid., 27).

Figure 1: The bunny poses in the author's dining room in Cambridge, Massachusetts (author's photo).

perplexed employee who probably didn't have the authority to engage in such a transaction and likely pocketed the đồng that we handed over. But that would be his story to tell to whatever audience he might convene. Perhaps he did so, or perhaps his story dissipated as the đồng entered his wallet and we returned to my friend's car. That moment, Mary's ability to delight in such a seemingly trivial or even ridiculous object without getting all caught up in apologizing for its frivolity, to be an appreciative audience for what the bunny had to say, that was Mary, and that was what Mary taught me.

When I returned from fieldwork, the bunny, carefully packed in lengths of hand-loomed textiles that I had collected, came home with me. I told the story to my husband as I unpacked, and I have repeated it whenever someone notices the bunny. The bunny's location has shifted over the years. Sometimes, it's been in my den, tucked away in a bookcase. At other times, it sits near me as I write, spurring me to find a voice and convene an audience. As I struggled to make sense of Mary's illness and death, the bunny moved to its present location in my dining room, which is both my current preferred writing space and the place in our house where convivial audiences sporadically congregate.

Since traveling halfway around the world from Vietnam to Cambridge, my ceramic bunny has become a homebody. It has left my apartment just once, in March 2018, when I carefully wrapped it in a towel, placed it in a bag from a recent AAS conference, and carried it down the street to Harvard's anthropology building, Tozzer, for a memorial gathering in Mary's honor. There, I told the bunny's origin story as I have reproduced it above, concluding my remarks by bringing that audience to the field on the outskirts of Ho Chi Minh City in 1995 to share the life lesson about audiencing that Mary had taught me.

Figure 2: The bunny visits the Harvard Anthropology Department, March 2018 (photo by Manduhai Buyandelger)

At some point in the story, I produced the bunny from a bag. I had intended to do so with a flourish, my version of a magician's rabbit from a hat, but the emotion of the moment meant that all I could muster was something more like an awkward gesture. I placed the bunny on a small table nearby (Figure 2). While I was speaking or shortly after I finished, I'm not sure which, a second bunny—Mary's bunny—appeared next to mine (Figure 3). Marianne Fritz, the anthropology department's graduate-program administrator, had fetched it from Mary's office. As Marianne said to the assembled group, the bunny had been in Mary's office for as long as she could remember. Marianne never knew what it meant, why it was there, or where it was from, but now she did. The bunnies stared at each other from tables across the room, as others continued telling stories about Mary.

Figure 3: Mary Steedly's bunny convenes an audience (L to R: Juno Salazar Parreñas, Marianne Fritz, and Ajantha Subramanian; photo by Manduhai Buyandelger)

Later that day, I emailed a brief report of the memorial gathering to a group that was planning an AAA (American Anthropological Association) roundtable in Mary's honor. One participant in that email exchange, Doreen Lee, who had also attended the gathering, wrote, "Ann Marie, thank you for the uncanny image of a field of white bunnies, export-oriented clones liberated by you and Mary!" Another attendee, Manduhai Buyandelger, wrote that she had arrived after I finished telling the story, but, seeing the interest in the bunnies, took pictures of them and the audiences they convened (Figures 2 and 3). Others wrote that they hoped they could hear the story at some point soon.

Having told the bunny story once, I had thought that would be that. I was scheduled to present on the keyword "audience" at the AAA roundtable in Mary's honor. There would be people there who had been at the Harvard gathering as well. My scholarly impulses warned me that audiencing might not bear repetition. Surely, I should come up with a new idea, an original story to pay tribute to Mary. But as a scholar whose work has focused in part on fashion, I know all too well the trap that lurked here, the allure of the next big thing that will satisfy and delight. And it does, until it doesn't.

As the day for the AAA roundtable drew closer, I realized the obvious: stories are not to be told just once and then evaporate. They are to be told again and again … and again and again. They are to be told in different ways to different audiences. And in the same ways to the same audiences. Stories matter because they are told and retold. I'm not sure what is cause and what is effect. Do we retell stories because we think they matter? Or do stories come to matter because they are retold? Heraclitian, a story and its audience are the flowing river that is never the same twice and yet is recognizable as that river. The act of engaging with story is performative and multisensory. As with the Indonesian nation, stories and their repetition enable us to imagine something into being together: that Mary visited me in the metaphorical field of fieldwork in which we found ourselves in a literal field of ceramic replicants. That Mary could validate my own sense of wonder in that bunny, in the uncanniness of its expression, its companions, and its position in that field. That Mary could then and can now, through this narrative and through this audience, help us to see that the bunny was a copy, yet it was unique, just like the stories about it and the audiences it has convened. Mary taught me about the intersociality and intersubjectivity that emerges when "audience" becomes "to audience." Thank you, my reader, for audiencing, so that we may continue to imagine Mary's legacy together.

SPECIFICITY

Juno Salazar Parreñas

My PhD advisor, Mary Margaret Steedly, posed a question to me during that rite of passage known as "the defense." Her commentary has guided me ever since, including during the years when I revised my thesis into a book. She discussed how I wrote about my human and nonhuman ethnographic subjects:

> I really like, Juno, the way that you ... were able to work both with orangutans as individuals and as kinds, that capacity to deal with different scales, let's say. I think that's really important and it's a little dangerous, because you do risk the accusation of anthropomorphizing, when you start giving them names. Is this Meerkat Manor as ethnography, where you start making up stories? I don't think you do, not at all. There's a very nice balance between the primatological issues that you are dealing with and the distinctive personalities of orangutans. You also do that with your human subjects. Instead of having kinds of collective identities, you were able to address them as people with specific issues and concerns and lifestyles and so on and I think that's really wonderful to put both of those together, and see what happens in those interactions, but it does seem to me in doing that, and you may be forced to do this, but it does seem that the larger structures in which these social relations are embedded tend to either dissolve or blur into generic categories of capitalism, neoliberalism, colonialism, without as much specificity as I'd like to see. And I don't even know if that is possible. You can't do everything. You can't focus on everything. But it does seem to me that it would be helpful to kind of engage more with the social context in which those interactions took place, *in a very specific way*: not just colonialism, but British colonialism in Sarawak, which is a very distinctive sort of thing. Not just indigenous peoples, but Ibans specifically. I'd just really like you to thicken up the context in which these

---

Juno Salazar Parreñas is an assistant professor of women's, gender, and sexuality studies at The Ohio State University.

were going on, a little bit. Because I think that if it didn't make it so confusing and complicated to figure anything out, it could possibly enrich what you are doing ...[1]

Mary's words come across as an invitation, one I'm free to take or leave. It's that very subtle push to specificity that made Mary's ethnographic method so powerfully honest, sincere, and rigorously empirical.[2] It's what makes her writing hold up beyond waves and turns. And it's something I hold onto even in the face of increased pressure to adopt and deploy terms like decolonial, decolonization, and the Anthropocene.

In the video of my defense, there's a moment where Mary draws me into a private conversation in this public space. What she has to say demands the attention of only the direct interlocutors and it does not beckon an audience. It's in this space of the side conversation that she gives her unfiltered and direct thoughts.

My committee member Steven Caton said that a story I told in the dissertation about Barbara Harrisson in the 1950s made the larger stakes of my project most clear to him. I enthusiastically agreed with his suggestion to put it at the beginning of the book manuscript. Once Steve began uncorking the champagne, Mary pulled me aside at that very moment to say that no way should I begin my book with a colonial white lady!

I took the advice of both committee members. My book starts with a female orangutan, but the first substantive chapter is mostly about a colonial white lady and the sources she left behind.[3] I have adopted Mary's insistence on the value of specificity and continue to take it in a literal direction with my ethnographic focus on interspecies and multispecies relations.[4] In this essay, I expand on that work to think about the weight of specificity as anchors to the thought bubbles generated by scholarly conversations. I do this by thinking about Harrisson's early orangutan rehabilitation efforts.

The goal of rehabilitation, both in the past and now, is to attain wildness. Yet the impact of human contact forever transforms orangutans, such that wildness is impossible. Rehabilitant orangutans are truly semi-wild. To me, the sense of semi-wild, as conveyed through the Malay word *bebas*, contains the experimental possibilities of decolonization. And these possibilities can erupt within the confines of colonial structures.

---

[1] I'm able to quote Mary verbatim, thanks to my sister, Maria Stalford, a fellow former doctoral student of Mary's, who did me the favor of videotaping my defense.

[2] Mary Margaret Steedly. *Hanging without a Rope: Narrative Experience in Colonial and Postcolonial Karoland* (Princeton: Princeton University Press, 1993). See also Mary Margaret Steedly, *Rifle Reports: A Story of Indonesian Independence* (Berkeley: University of California Press, 2013).

[3] Juno Salazar Parreñas, *Decolonizing Extinction: The Work of Care in Orangutan Rehabilitation* (Durham: Duke University Press, 2018).

[4] For the concept of multispecies relations, see Anna Tsing, *Friction: An Ethnography of Global Connection* (Princeton: Princeton University Press, 2005). For interspecies relations, see Julie Livingston and Jasbir K. Puar, "Interspecies," *Social Text* 29, 1 (106) (Spring 2011): 3–14. In addition to orangutan rehabilitation efforts, I have written about Southeast Asian volunteer tourism involving endemic species, specifically Asian elephants in Thailand and Bornean orangutans in Malaysia, and am working on a new project about the emergence of "animal retirement" around the world when human retirement is perceived as a crisis in the very same places.

Mary signed the center of my poster for my defense with the wish, "May you stay semi-wild." I have come to interpret this as a piece of playful and yet sage advice. I interpret it as a reminder that, even when experiencing a state of arrest within my own institutionalized life, there remain possibilities for resistance and liberation.

Harrisson's memoir *Orang Utan* was published in 1962, a year before Sarawak was incorporated into the federal state of Malaysia and officially decolonized.[5] Harrisson distances her household and by extension herself from the hegemony of the colonial bourgeoisie. This is especially conveyed through the look of her home. She explains that her dwelling was "the housewife's bad dream, a conglomeration of all things Bornean, pinned and stuck on wall and ceiling, lying on tables and floor everywhere and nowhere."[6] Her aesthetics stood in contrast to "lady visitors of orthodox tastes" who would enter her home and either be too shocked to speak or they would exclaim, "how can you *live* here?"[7] Through her portrayal of such visitors, Harrisson rejects the civilizing authority of British colonial femininity.[8]

As the interior spaces of her home rejected Western civilization and celebrated Sarawak's diversities instead, the same sentiment echoed through the "green wilderness" of the bungalow's exterior.[9] It was not severely controlled European landscaping, nor the cultivated flourishing of an English garden.[10] Instead, it was as Sarawakian as the rest of the house: durian trees, pineapple bushes, frangipani, and hibiscus. It was technically not "wild," because her descriptions consisted of cultivars, which are by definition domesticated. Yet at Bunglo Segu they had a life of their own. Harrisson suggests that their feral growth was made possible by the "sporadic" quality of human interventions on the land.[11] This, too, stood in clear contrast to the gardens of Borneo's swidden agriculturalists, whose carefully managed plots growing rattan and durian trees are often misunderstood by outsiders as abandoned or laid to waste.[12] Harrisson's feral garden mirrored the feral futures for which she hoped on behalf of the orangutans she raised, like Eve.

Eve looked frighteningly malnourished. She was just seven pounds when she came under Harrisson's care, despite having teeth that indicated an age of almost one year. It might have been the sight of Eve's emaciation or the chafe marks on Eve's neck from a chain that left the skin raw that compelled Harrisson's housekeeper, Dayang, to say the following to Harrisson:

---

[5] Barbara Harrisson, *Orang-Utan* (London: Collins, 1962).

[6] Barbara Harrisson, *Orang-Utan* (Singapore: Oxford University Press, 1987), 32.

[7] Harrisson, *Orang-Utan* (1987), 32.

[8] Antoinette Burton, *Burdens of History: British Feminists, Indian Women, and Imperial Culture, 1865–1915* (Chapel Hill: University of North Carolina Press, 1994).

[9] Harrisson, *Orang-Utan* (1987), 32

[10] Yi-Fu Tuan, *Dominance and Affection: The Making of Pets* (New Haven: Yale University Press, 1984). See also Keith Thomas, *Man and the Natural World: Changing Attitudes in England, 1500–1800* (New York: Oxford University Press, 1996).

[11] Harrisson, *Orang-Utan* (1987), 32.

[12] Stephanie Gordon Fried, "Tropical Forests Forever? A Contextual Ecology of Bentian Rattan Agroforestry Systems," In *People, Plants, and Justice: The Politics of Nature Conservation*, ed. Charles Zerner (New York: Columbia University Press, 2000).

"She is surely small, Mem, she must take milk or she will die—let me try and take her." With a sigh of relief, I [Harrisson] handed her over, hoping that Dayang at last had found what she missed so much in our household: a baby to cuddle and look after.[13]

Dayang's apparent wish for her employers to have children could have stemmed from a wish to secure her own employment.[14] Yet Harrisson appears to have understood Dayang's tenderness as a representation of a sympathetic human motherhood, in which feeding and cuddling are crucial for the survival of the desperately dependent baby.

Harrisson expresses a form of care that she implicitly contrasts with Dayang's. She echoes the science of motherhood popularized in guidebooks written by practitioners of newly professionalized Western medicine in the first half of the twentieth century.[15] Readers of Harrisson's memoir are shown the failure of Dayang's vision of motherly tenderness. Harrisson writes, "Eve refused to drink and Dayang registered despair: 'She will die, Mem, you will see!'"[16] Eve's refusal prompted Harrisson to follow a new course of action and pursue a new way of becoming. Harrisson describes using a glass pipette to force-feed Eve. Force-feeding is an act of violent domination intended to end protest and force life.[17]

I wonder: When facing the possibility of an orangutan dying right in your presence, what would you do? Would you intervene by force-feeding, as Harrisson did? Or would you let the orangutan die, perhaps yielding to the orangutan's agency, as Dayang probably would have done? The men I knew who train orangutans, in a way, perform rehabilitation as acts of forced feeding: they would whack the orangutans with sticks, but felt that the cruelty of hurting an orangutan so that the orangutan would be averse to human contact was fully justified. Being kept alive in punitive circumstances of the wildlife center, these orangutans at least had a chance to live at all. The women employed at orangutan rehabilitation centers whom I met through fieldwork appear to try an alternative, where they turn their bodies away or rub their wrists with eucalyptus oil so that if an orangutan tries to get near them, they recoil from the sting in their eyes. Such a practice is a third way akin to force-feeding but with less force, encouraging displaced orangutans to survive and thrive with a little less violence in their lives. I wonder about a fourth way: What would it be like to come to terms with Eve's death and the death of her species?

Coming to terms with death is processual: the phrase "coming to terms" remains an active verb in the present participle, arrested in a movement between becoming and

---

[13] Harrisson, *Orang-Utan* (1987), 37–38.

[14] Ann Laura Stoler and Karen Strassler, "Castings for the Colonial: Memory Work in 'New Order' Java," *Comparative Studies in Society and History* 42, 1 (2000): 4–48.

[15] Childrearing guidebooks shifted the authority of mothering from networks of experienced women to trained medical experts. See Nancy Pottishman Weiss, "Mother, the Invention of Necessity: Dr. Benjamin Spock's Baby and Child Care," *American Quarterly* 29, 5 (1977): 519–46.

[16] Harrisson, *Orang-Utan* (1987), 38.

[17] For the politics of force-feeding and force-feeding as a form of torture, see: Herman Reyes, "Force-feeding and Coercion: No Physician Complicity," *Virtual Mentor: American Medical Association Journal of Ethics* 9, 10 (October 2007): 5; and Laleh Khalili, *Time in the Shadows: Confinement in Counterinsurgencies* (Stanford: Stanford University Press, 2013).

ending. I still do not know what coming to terms with Mary's death actually would be. I wish I could talk with her and think with her depth of knowledge that she quietly kept and would only share once I expressed to her my superficial grasp of concepts like *sakit hati*.[18] The memory of her careful specificity, so crucial for her nuanced analysis, continues to guide me.

When Mary advised that I stay semi-wild, I knew that she, too, was semi-wild. The weight of Harvard's red-brick and white-concrete walls never seemed to weigh her down or make her stodgy. She was open to ideas, agile of mind like her sporty dogs were agile on the field. She rejected the pressure to produce a factory of rehashed ideas and instead thought deeply, creatively, and without the constraint of discipline. She never let her institution define her. Within her institutional constraints, she was able to foster our wild ideas, cultivate the creativity of our narratives, and enable us to think deeply about things that may have seemed simple, but were always complicated and especially worth figuring out.

---

[18] In January 2011, Mary read the first draft of my narration of a particularly eventful incident. I wrote that the orangutan Ching was angry (*sakit hati*). Mary thankfully brought to my attention that my explanation was far too simple, that the term had much deeper meaning. She told me that *sakit hati* is not just about being angry, but about being wronged and suffering injustice. Her passion for understanding cultural concepts specific to Indonesia and *Nusantara* was profound.

NATIONALISM

Veronika Kusumaryati

It is impossible to talk about Mary Margaret Steedly without talking about Indonesia, an archipelagic nation that is an actual physical entity but also a political project. As Clifford Geertz says, "Places are accidents and their names ideas," and that is how field sites are made for many anthropologists.[1] Mary's interest in Indonesia, however, endured, not only in her research but also her teaching. At Harvard, she almost singlehandedly advised a number of Indonesian students, me being one of them.

Mary first went to Indonesia in the 1980s, when I was just a child in a rural village in Yogyakarta. Neither of my parents went to college, but they have a fairly liberal orientation. In Yogyakarta, this means quiet resistance to the orthodoxy and conformity of Javanese cultures. My parents never forced me to speak high or middle Javanese at home. They also never expressed any interest to work for the government—an aspiration that almost every Javanese villager has, at least in Yogyakarta, for government employees are "the aristocracy," *priyayi*. After becoming a Golkar (Partai Golongan Karya, Party of Functional Groups) cadre for a few years, my father decided to shift his political allegiance to the PDI (Partai Demokrasi Indonesia, Indonesian Democratic Party) in the late 1980s. My mother, who tended to be better read, had always had an ambivalent relationship with the regime, though she was actively involved in and championed various government programs, like family planning. Indeed, every Indonesian citizen at that time had to participate actively in

---

Veronika Kusumaryati, a postdoctoral fellow in Harvard University's department of anthropology, presented an early version of this essay on December 1, 2018, at the Harvard symposium "Other Voices, Other Stories: Mary Margaret Steedly's Ethnographic Legacies." The author is grateful to the organizers of the conference, and she also thanks Karen Strassler, Patricia Spyer, Smita Lahiri, and Namita Dharia for their comments on a draft of the article.

[1] Clifford Geertz, *After the Fact: Two Countries, Four Decades, One Anthropologist* (Cambridge: Harvard University Press, 1995), 22.

various government programs, from taking classes and tutorials in the state ideology of Pancasila to carrying out *gotong royong* (communal work) for infrastructure projects.

Unbeknown to most of us on Java, the 1970s and '80s were marked by a violent consolidation of the New Order regime in Indonesia's peripheral regions, especially after a brutal colonial invasion of East Timor in 1975, the designation of West Papua as an area of military operation (or *Daerah Operasi Militer*, DOM) in 1977, and the suppression of the Free Aceh Movement from 1976 to 1979. Thus, while it can seem that the New Order's hegemony went unchallenged domestically and internationally, dissent was everywhere. Grassroot movements and nongovernmental organizations (NGOs) began to emerge. Dissatisfaction began to be expressed more explicitly. To return to my father, he decided to leave Golkar after his involvement in a small demonstration demanding that the government extend electricity lines to his district. I am not sure how intense the political experience was for him, but he started to listen to the Indonesian broadcasts of the BBC and Australian radio, which offered different perspectives from regular Indonesian broadcasts. Through these media, we heard about the Kedung Ombo Dam case, wherein several high-profile Catholic pastors actively supported the resistance against the construction of the dam—my father is a Catholic. We also heard about the killing of *preman* ("suspected criminals"), which began in Yogyakarta and spread across Indonesia.[2]

Mary rarely talked about her 1980's fieldwork experience, even though she constantly talked about the food in Medan. Yet her ethnography based on that research spoke to quiet forms of resistance and partial incorporation into New Order projects in ways that resonate with my own family's relationship to the state. An atmosphere of coercion, violence, and abuse of power is palpably felt in her work, even if it remains mostly at the periphery of her account. Like my parents and so many others during the New Order, the Karo Batak she wrote about did not so much openly resist as live at an oblique angle to the authoritarian regime.

Mary's interest in North Sumatra might have been an "accident," as Geertz has it,[3] or a result of practical considerations, but in the larger scheme of Indonesian studies at that time, it was unique. If her fieldwork in Indonesia coincided with the consolidation of New Order rule, in the United States it took place during the consolidation of Indonesian studies as a respectable field. Emerging right after World War II, American scholarship on Southeast Asia focused attention on new nation-states recently independent from European and Japanese colonialism. The arrival of the nation-state as a new political community in the region and the shift from European colonial scholarship to American scholarship also led to an examination of the processes of modernization and cultural change. This tendency followed the dominant American post-war social science paradigm and had an ideological underpinning in the US agenda in Southeast Asia, namely, to offer an American way to modernity.[4] Such scholarship was also marked by the primacy of the study of culture and the dominant

---

[2] J. Van der Kroef. "'Petrus': Patterns of Prophylactic Murder in Indonesia," *Asian Survey* 25, 7 (1985): 745–59.

[3] Geertz, *After the Fact*, 22.

[4] Victor King and William D. Wilder, eds., *The Modern Anthropology of South-East Asia: An Introduction* (New York: Routledge, 2003), 72.

role of interpretive anthropology in studying Southeast Asian societies as best represented by Clifford Geertz and, in my argument, Hildred Geertz.

Few anthropologists worked in North Sumatra before—and after—Mary. From the United States, these include Edward M. Bruner, Susan Rodgers, Rita Smith Kipp, and Ann Laura Stoler.[5] At that time, the dominant trend of Indonesian studies mainly focused on Java. George M. Kahin, Benedict Anderson, James Siegel, John Pemberton, Claire Holt, and a few others who worked at Cornell or Yale were interested in Indonesian politics, while the University of Chicago's Clifford Geertz, who started his fieldwork in Indonesia in the late 1950s, examined Indonesia's prospects for modernization.

Mary read Geertz's works during her graduate years at the University of Michigan and worked as his research assistant at Princeton's Institute of Advanced Studies from 1988 to 1989. When I was in my second year of graduate school and just learning how to be an anthropologist—Mary had persuaded me to come to Harvard after reading part of my undergraduate thesis on Indonesian horror film—she recalled that every week she would have lunch with Geertz and talk about her research. She always admired him as a writer.

In 2011, I was in my second year of graduate studies and was just learning how to be an anthropologist when she persuaded me to come to Harvard. Mary included some of Clifford Geertz's works in her syllabi, but it was Hildred Geertz whom she urged me to read for my general exams. Mary and Hildred seem to share similar interests in visual arts and cultures as an "urban superstructure," not to mention that both were good fieldworkers. Indeed, it is clear from this and Mary's classes at Harvard that, for her, anthropology offers ethnography as a distinctive genre of writing and, concomitantly, fieldwork as a specific way of knowing the world. For her, fieldwork is not only the *sine qua non* of modern anthropology, the ritual initiation experience in the discipline, but also the source of anthropological theory. But what kind of anthropological theory did Mary develop?

In her first book, she writes about Karo people's conception of [his]stories and the potential of ethnography to reveal these historical narratives as a construct. She examines how unofficial histories resist the power of absorption into and exclusion from official history in the context of Karo encounters with the modern world via colonialism and especially Indonesian nationalism.[6] Her second book in particular examines Karo people's conceptions of national history through their accounts of the revolution in Karoland, 1945–49. Nationalism has been one of the major strands of scholarship in Indonesian studies, especially for Yale and Cornell scholars. However, Mary's work in North Sumatra complicates the predominant idea of Indonesian nationalism and its Java-centric orientation in three key ways. First, her field study of the Christian Karo shows how the Karo understood Indonesia and Indonesian nationalism differently from the elite, male, Javanese nationalists who constituted the

---

[5] Some Dutch anthropologists worked during the colonial and postcolonial period, while Masri Singarimbun was the only native anthropologist who conducted extended research in Karo.

[6] Mary Margaret Steedly, *Hanging without a Rope: Narrative Experience in Colonial and Postcolonial Karoland* (Princeton: Princeton University Press, 1993), 238.

principal subjects in many studies of Indonesian nationalism.[7] Scholars working outside Java frequently use the term "modernity" to refer to their subjects' complicated engagements with the nation, pointing to their uncertain loyalties and unstable location within the imagination of the Indonesian nation.[8] Like Indonesia itself, Indonesianists like Mary have struggled to incorporate non-Javanese, Christian, animist, poor, and rural women and men and their perspectives into the discussion of Indonesian nationalism. But what Mary showed articulately was that the project of the nation has been always colored by not only a sense of uncertain loyalty but also, and most explicitly, exclusion. Like her Karo subjects, Mary was interested in "[a] sense of ambivalent national belonging," a story of nationalism that comes from "the outskirts of the nation" and histories that are embedded in the local.[9] Thus, Mary's works not only decenter the dominant narrative of Indonesian nationalism, as Dwyer puts it, but also resist a strong tendency within Indonesian studies to "fetishize" the New Order and Java, or to use Java as a substitute for Indonesia.[10] Her works also reflect not only the limit of Indonesian nationalism or nationalism, but also reveal "the way that nationalism is not necessarily a liberating project."[11] Mary recognized that nationalism has its own attractive power without assuming that those who participate in it so passionately are the ideologically committed subjects imagined in dominant nationalist discourses and official history.

Second, the location not only constitutes and determines Mary's [situated] knowledge. She also considers the Karo themselves as an *epistemic community*, as historical actors who articulate what it means to be part of a supralocal entity called Indonesia. Thus, her extensive interviews and oral histories among the Karo and specifically Karo women were not only an anthropological method to make sense of history, but also to recognize the fact that historical reconstruction is a narrative construction that is subject to heteroglossia, to various voicings and the question of power. Here, her ethnography should also be read as one of these constructions, not as a direct translation of her fieldwork experience. Her text is a result of "dialogue," "conventions of narrative plausibility," and "social space and sociality" that her text inhabits.[12] This is where her feminist scholarship intervenes most forcefully. Her use of

---

[7] Some examples are: Harry Benda, *Decolonization in Indonesia: The Problem of Continuity and Change* (New Haven: Yale University Southeast Asia Studies, 1965) and *Continuity and Change in Southeast Asia* (New Haven: Yale University Southeast Asia Studies, 1972); Benedict Anderson, *Imagined Communities: Reflections on the Origin and Spread of Nationalism* (London: Verso, 1983); James T. Siegel, *Solo in the New Order: Language and Hierarchy in an Indonesian City* (Princeton: Princeton University Press, 1986) and *A New Criminal Type in Jakarta* (Durham: Duke University Press, 1998); and Hans Pols, *Nurturing Indonesia: Medicine and Decolonisation in the Dutch East Indies* (New York: Cambridge University Press, 2018).

[8] See: Janet Hoskins, *The Play of Time: Kodi Perspectives on Calendars, History, and Exchange* (Berkeley: University of California Press, 1993); Patricia Spyer, *The Memory of Trade: Modernity's Entanglements on an Eastern Indonesian Island* (Durham: Duke University Press, 2000); Webb Keane, "Public Speaking: On Indonesian As the Language of the Nation," *Public Culture* 15, 3 (2003): 503–30; and Danilyn Rutherford, *Raiding the Land of the Foreigners: The Limits of the Nation on an Indonesian Frontier* (Princeton: Princeton University Press, 2003).

[9] Mary Margaret Steedly, *Rifle Reports: A Story of Indonesian Independence* (Berkeley: University of California Press, 2013), 8.

[10] Leslie Dwyer, "Review Essay II" in "Reviewed Work(s): *Rifle Reports: A Story of Indonesian Independence*, by Mary Margaret Steedly," *Sojourn* 30, 3 (November 2015): 863–69.

[11] Karen Strassler, personal communication.

[12] Steedly, *Rifle Reports*, 9.

the term "narrative experience" attempts to tackle the situatedness of the narrative and what it tells us about Karo experiences. This is a positioning and location-work that is sensitive to "the contingency of the nation form, the nature of the state, and the difficulty of aligning local and national worlds of belonging."[13] This attitude is allowed by her strong commitment to feminist epistemology that manifests in her conception of gendered nationalism. This is her major contribution to the study of Indonesian nationalism and, broadly, to the study of nationalism.[14]

Third, Mary's scholarship on Indonesian nationalism is also shaped by her complicated conceptualization of the condition of postcoloniality. Mary did not see independence as the end of colonialism. Postcoloniality is not a rupture but, rather, "a recurrent history."[15] At Harvard she taught a course entitled "Colonial Departures," which argued that the postcolonial future is "made not necessarily as they [the colonized] wished," but always bears "a complex relation to the residual forms and ruins of colonial rule."[16] While scholars have paid attention to the shift from colonialism to postcoloniality, Mary examines the historical fissure left by the departure of European power and the social revolution and violence internal to the Indonesian revolution. This period of revolution (1945–49) sits uneasily within the militarized nationalist historiography of Indonesia, especially as the period was marked by ideological battles among different factions comprising Indonesian nationalists, including various paramilitary groups, Islamic organizations, and the Communist Party. The militarized history of Indonesian nationalism not only does not give a place for many of these groups, especially the Communists, but it also erases them. In addition, the messiness and internal violence of Indonesian revolution do not conform with the heroic nationalist accounts of the revolution as a unified "struggle" led by the Indonesian army. Accounts like Mary's not only complicate but fundamentally challenge militarized Indonesian nationalist history. On the other hand, Mary's historiography also questions official Dutch accounts of the Dutch return as police actions—a position until recently echoed in Dutch historiography.

These aspects of her work inform how I examine Indonesia—as an Indonesian working in the United States. It is not a coincidence that she urged me to choose between West Papua and East Timor for my fieldwork. I never asked her why she was so interested in East Timor or West Papua, but in retrospect it seems clear. Both of us are interested in looking at the Indonesian nation from the margin, the outskirts, or even the outside.

It is still true that Indonesia has become a paradigmatic place in which nationalism is understood and theorized,[17] that Indonesian nationalism still inspires many

---

[13] Steedly, *Rifle Reports*, 17.

[14] See: Smita Lahiri, "On Nonrecognition and Feminist Epistemology: Doing Ethnographic Theory with Mary Steedly," *EASA Network of Ethnographic Theory*, January 2019, https://networkofethnographictheory.wordpress.com/on-nonrecognition-and-feminist-epistemology-doing-ethnographic-theory-with-mary-steedly/; and Benedict Anderson, Leslie Dwyer, and Mary M. Steedly, "Reviewed Work(s)," *Sojourn* 30, 3 (2015): 860–76.

[15] Ann Laura Stoler, *Duress: Imperial Durabilities in Our Times* (Durham: Duke University Press, 2016).

[16] She planned to teach this class in the spring of 2016, but canceled it due to her deteriorating health.

[17] Contemporary scholarship on Indonesian nationalism includes: Karen Strassler, *Refracted Visions: Popular Photography and National Modernity in Java* (Durham: Duke University Press, 2010); and Doreen Lee, *Activist Archives: Youth Culture and the Political Past in Indonesia* (Durham: Duke University Press, 2016).

Indonesians to defend against those who are considered disloyal or commit treason (*makar*)—mainly non-Javanese Indonesians. But the fall of the New Order's authoritarian regime shaped the way in which my generation thinks about Indonesia as a political project. For one, the state-centered history no longer holds its hegemonic power, as democracy and new digital technology, among other things, have arrived and changed the way in which history can be accessed. Many of us no longer dwell on the memory of *perjuangan* (national struggle). A lot of us still do, of course, like the Karo, participate passionately in the dramatic enactment of the nation. In West Papua, where I work as an anthropologist, I found not only ambivalence, but also a refusal to accept Indonesia's claim to history and nationhood as well as a struggle to enact a nationalism of their own—Papuan nationalism. This proves that Indonesia still offers the possibility to rethink nationalism, colonialism, and postcolonialism in new ways.

OUTSKIRTS

Jesse Hession Grayman

To prepare this short piece, I reread the sections I highlighted in Mary Steedly's book *Rifle Reports*, which was published shortly after I completed my doctorate under her supervision.[1] My notes persistently remind me that Mary's approach to reading and interpreting narrative has profoundly influenced the way I approach ethnography. In what follows, I share two unsettling and unsettled ethnographic fragments from my research on post-conflict humanitarian interventions in Aceh that owe a debt of gratitude to what I have learned over the years from Mary's method of scholarship. Throughout I adopt the key word "outskirts" from *Rifle Reports* to comment upon not just the status of post-conflict Aceh within the Indonesian nation, but also the unusual methodologies my fieldwork required, and the importance of uncertain, ambiguous narratives to complicate tidy histories of Aceh's recovery from catastrophes both natural and man-made.

Aceh province is just over the northern border from where Mary did her research in Karoland, in North Sumatra province, which she called the "outskirts of the nation," at the northwest corner of Sumatra island, and all of Indonesia. The outskirts are not just geographically distant from the metropolitan center, but also fraught with "ambivalent national belonging ... simultaneously incorporated and marginalized" into the national Indonesian community.[2] The people of Aceh not only made crucial contributions to Indonesia's nationalist narrative of anticolonial struggle and the revolutionary war for independence, thus securing an essential place in the national imaginary, but they have also lived through multiple secession movements, suffering

---

Jesse Hession Grayman is a senior lecturer in development studies at the University of Auckland's School of Social Sciences.

[1] Mary Margaret Steedly, *Rifle Reports: A Story of Indonesian Independence* (Berkeley: University of California Press, 2013).

[2] Steedly, *Rifle Reports*, 8.

incomprehensibly violent counterinsurgency operations by Indonesian security forces.[3] One of the first insights I take away from *Rifle Reports* is that this model of counterinsurgency was set, the die was cast, during Indonesia's revolutionary war when the young republican army consolidated itself over less organized or competitor militia groups, creating terror and uncertainty alongside nationalist fervor.

My ethnographic research examines post-conflict recovery efforts in Aceh after the Indonesian government signed a peace agreement with the Free Aceh Movement in August 2005, which brought an end to nearly three decades of Aceh's ethno-nationalist secession movement and Indonesia's counterinsurgency. My dissertation focuses on the young, educated Acehnese-Indonesians who were involved in this work, many employed through international humanitarian organizations.[4] These organizations were already present in Aceh and available to begin post-conflict recovery work, as they were heavily involved in rehabilitation and reconstruction efforts after the December 2004 Indian Ocean earthquake and tsunami that killed more than 180,000 people and decimated hundreds of kilometers of Aceh's coastline. After the tragic twin disasters of conflict and tsunami, the recovery period was an exciting time. Many of my colleagues and informants enthusiastically pursued the work of peace building and recovery in Aceh, grateful that their contributions to civil society—including a few activists who returned to Aceh after the peace agreement guaranteed their safety— were recognized, and their work rewarded with generous salaries. They had compelling stories to tell, and so did the beneficiaries of the projects they implemented, including survivors of violence, amnestied political prisoners, and former combatants.

While employed with these humanitarian organizations, I found myself in the unusual position, for an anthropology doctoral student, of working on large research projects, training and managing dozens of field researchers, and leading provincial-wide studies instead of more traditional village-based or other local-level field research. It was difficult to analyze narrative data, particularly when I was working with transcripts for interviews that I had not conducted myself. For instance, one project I worked on forbade foreigners from directly interacting with conflict survivors. On others, I found it difficult to interview rural women. The validity of these interviews might also be questioned when many of them were conducted on behalf of large donors and government agencies. How does one engage with these data ethnographically, or as *Rifle Reports* posits, "to dwell on context as well as text, to circle around the written, translated words of the transcript, and to fill in the gaps of implicit social meaning, local knowledge, and cultural *poiesis*—or, at the very least, to recognize the absence of these"?[5] I wondered if I might have to settle for recognizing absence.

---

[3] See, for example: Anthony Reid, ed., *Verandah of Violence: The Background to the Aceh Problem* (Singapore: Singapore University Press, 2006); Edward Aspinall, *Islam and Nation: Separatist Rebellion in Aceh, Indonesia* (Stanford: Stanford University Press, 2009); Tim Kell, *The Roots of Acehnese Rebellion, 1989–1992* (Ithaca: Cornell Modern Indonesia Project—Southeast Asia Program, 1995); Geoffrey Robinson, "Rawan is as Rawan Does: The Origins of Disorder in New Order Aceh," *Indonesia* 66 (1998): 127–57; and Jesse Hession Grayman, Mary-Jo Delvecchio Good, and Byron J Good, "Conflict Nightmares and Trauma in Aceh," *Culture Medicine & Psychiatry* 33, 2 (2009): 290–312.

[4] Jesse Hession Grayman, "Humanitarian Encounters in Post-Conflict Aceh, Indonesia" (doctoral dissertation, Harvard University Graduate School of Arts and Sciences, Department of Anthropology, 2013).

[5] Steedly, *Rifle Reports*, 30.

For a semester back in Cambridge, in 2010, I sat in on Mary's "Ethnography as Practice and Genre" class at Harvard. When it was my turn to share a piece of writing, I projected onto the screen a short profile I had written about a female ex-combatant from the Free Aceh Movement whom I named Dona. The writing was flat, like most NGO reports. I felt my face turn white as my work was met with blank stares. For a moment, I was mortified, but it started a conversation about what it is like to meet someone on paper. Where do I fit into the narrative if I was not even present for the interview? What compels me to bring Dona's story into my dissertation?

The answer is that I was touched by her songs. Dona wrote songs for her friends while she was in prison, and she sang them for her interviewer, who then transcribed the lyrics and later intensively worked on translations with me. These lyrics, for instance, combine the apocalyptic imageries of Aceh's war and tsunami, bundling them into a love narrative:

The neck was slit and brought to the beach

The blood poured out like a heavy rain

Oh Lord the man I loved is no longer here

It felt as if the Earth quaked at the moment Cut Bang died

My life carries on without direction anymore [6]

I used this and other material to write a chapter titled "Remote Fieldwork," a meditation on these heterodox ethnographic methods. This provided opportunities to reflect upon the uncanny moments of perceived intimacy with informants I never met, such as Dona, and, alternatively, the awkward distance sometimes generated in face to face conversations, as my second example, below, shows.[7] These insights came directly out of discussions in Mary's seminar room, and I might just have easily titled the chapter "Ethnography on the Outskirts" to acknowledge the ambivalent commitments some contemporary anthropologists have with older ideas about their signature method, fieldwork.[8]

Once you start paying attention to the layered moments of the interview, the moment of transcription and translation, and the moment of interpreting texts, whole new modes of analysis and insight open up. Later in my thesis, I worked through a set of ideas across two chapters in which I argue that many of my informants who worked for international humanitarian organizations were finding new ways to think of themselves as both Acehnese and Indonesian again.[9] My data validated much of what anthropologist James Siegel had argued previously, that the conflict had foreclosed the

---

[6] Dona's (not her real name) story and direct quotations are drawn from interview transcript B.45 in the archival materials used for Jesse Hession Grayman, "Community Perceptions of the Peace Process: Eleven Case Studies for the Multi-Stakeholder Review of Post-Conflict Programming in Aceh (MSR)" (report for the World Bank, 2009).

[7] Grayman, "Humanitarian Encounters in Post-Conflict Aceh," 136–62 (chapter two, "Remote Fieldwork").

[8] Akhil Gupta and James Ferguson, "Discipline and Practice: 'The Field' as Site, Method, and Location in Anthropology," in *Anthropological Locations: Boundaries and Grounds of a Field Science*, ed. Akhil Gupta and James Ferguson (Berkeley: University of California Press, 1997), 1–46.

[9] See: Grayman, "Humanitarian Encounters in Post-Conflict Aceh," 194–236 (chapter four, "Recognition") and 237–97 (chapter five, "Humanitarian Subjects").

possibilities of being both, but I also found that the humanitarian encounter after the tsunami and conflict opened new possibilities for Acehnese to reimagine their relationship with the Indonesian state.[10] Nonetheless, there are fragments in my data that resist the argument I was developing.

In early 2012, I was concluding a visit to South Aceh during which I interviewed the people I used to work with from 2005–08 at the International Organization for Migration (IOM). Shortly before I caught an overnight bus back to Banda Aceh, I was interviewing Sami Akmal, who worked with me at IOM on a variety of research projects. When I first met Sami in 2006, he was still trying to finish college. In 1999, Sami's higher education was interrupted, first by his busy activism in Aceh's student-led referendum movement and, second, by the consequences of his activism, when a police officer confiscated his ID and threatened his life. Shortly after surviving that close call, the police came looking for him at his boarding house in Banda Aceh, prompting Sami to drop out from school and activism until after the tsunami, when he could negotiate a rehabilitation of his identity and police record. By the time of our interview in 2012, Sami's local roots in South Aceh and his experience working on IOM's recovery projects for conflict-affected communities positioned him well for a political career in South Aceh's government. As Sami explained his plans, I marveled at another example of a young Acehnese man's trajectory into the middle class, once interrupted by violence, then resumed during Aceh's humanitarian encounter.

My friend Alfan interrupted my interview with Sami when he drove into the yard with someone we had never met before. Alfan took me aside: "Here's the story ... this guy is from my grandmother's village. He once met with someone from the United Nations Refugee Agency [UNHCR, United Nations High Commissioner for Refugees] in Malaysia. Now he wants to talk to you, just ask a few questions. Is that all right? It's nothing, really, let's just give him a little change of scenery." Curious, but cautious, I knew that UNHCR had a role managing conflict refugees from Aceh in Malaysia. UNHCR played only a brief and limited role in Aceh's tsunami recovery effort precisely because the Indonesian government condemned the organization's role in internationalizing the conflict, drawing attention to what Indonesia considered a domestic issue, by processing and resettling Aceh conflict victims who escaped to Malaysia. This man, whom I call Junaid, surely had some interesting stories to tell, but I also knew from experience that Junaid had probably gone out of his way to meet with me because he expected something I could not offer.

When I first asked his name, and to tell me something about himself, Junaid did not speak, but rather handed over two expired immigration cards from the Malaysian government. I observed Junaid's age, mid-thirties, which meant that he was in his mid-late twenties when he fled to Malaysia shortly after President Megawati declared martial law in Aceh in May 2003. He would not tell me whether he was an active (or mistaken, or deserting) member of the Free Aceh Movement trying to save his life, or an economic refugee disguised as an asylum seeker hoping for employment in the more prosperous, neighboring country. He returned to Aceh in early 2008, when Malaysia's temporary residence permits for Acehnese exiles officially expired. When Junaid spoke, he stammered through an abbreviated story of his exile, with repetitive

---

[10] James T. Siegel, *The Rope of God* (Ann Arbor: University of Michigan Press, 2000), 336–422 ("Possessed").

questions and refrains, in a thick acquired Malaysian accent mixed with a characteristic Acehnese style of using context-dependent shifters whose references are hardly clear. After Sami's expert chronological narrative, attuned specifically to answer all my questions, Junaid presented a difficult and awkward challenge for both of us.

"Before these cards were issued," he explained, "during the conflict, the UN gave us a white card. I want to ask about this. Mister, are you connected with UNHCR?" I explained that my employment history in Aceh never included a United Nations organization. After several unsuccessful attempts to place me with the UN, Junaid arrived at the crux of the matter:

> I wanted to ask about this, because when we were in Malaysia, the UNHCR official asked us, "when you return to Aceh, if it is safe to return, how can we help?" So when we got back to Aceh, was there any assistance from them, was there any? We were never able to find out, you see? That's what we want to know, was there anything or not? Because he asked us a long time ago ... So we came back here, but by that time, he had already left ... We could see all the signs from UNHCR [branding logos] from all their [post-tsunami] assistance. But we who held their cards, we didn't get anything.

Junaid continued repeating his main points ("I came back here, but they were gone," "card holders received nothing when they came home"), but woven through, new details and complaints emerged. He described UNHCR's rigorous interview to determine his refugee status when he first arrived in Malaysia. He told me the UNHCR card was a sign of international protection, "it protected those of us caught up in the conflict." He still hoped UNHCR would make good on its promise to assist after he returned home, and wanted me to explain how this might happen.

I tried another line of inquiry to break Junaid's repetitive, dispiriting questions: had Junaid ever pursued redress through the provincial government's Aceh Reintegration Agency (Badan Reintegrasi Aceh, BRA), set up to manage the reintegration of ex-combatants and conflict survivors? His answer, still saturated with yearning for UNHCR's return, provides a stark contrast against Sami's confident future:

> Since UNHCR left, I'm not sure. It's supposed to be safe here now, but we've been hearing about these shootings in Banda Aceh lately, so is it really safe? For the people who hold this card, the government makes it sound as if we brought information outside the country, because they know UNHCR asked us about intimidation [and other human rights violations in Aceh]. Better not look for trouble ... It's OK, better not look for trouble, better if we just stay calm.

In 2008, my research team interviewed a Free Aceh Movement ex-combatant who spent time in Malaysia as a refugee and proudly showed his expired UNHCR card. He told us "it was more dangerous to carry a UNHCR refugee card than to carry a weapon because [the Indonesian government] was afraid that Aceh would become an international issue, an embarrassment to Indonesia."[11] This is the danger that prevented Junaid from seeking redress from BRA. When Junaid says "better not look for trouble," he prefers to avoid recognition from the government. Like many others in

---

[11] Jesse Hession Grayman, "Official and Unrecognized Narratives of Recovery in Post Conflict Aceh, Indonesia," *Critical Asian Studies* 48, 4 (2016): 528–55.

the Aceh diaspora, Junaid seems stuck in the conflict era, when "no Indonesian authority held the confidence of the Acehnese," partly because he missed out on Aceh's transitional humanitarian encounter.[12] The UNHCR logos on the physical structures they built are all that remains of the organization he hoped would keep its promise to him. Junaid's uncertain condition, evident to me in his stammer and repetition, clinging to a Malaysian accent, suggests a political subjectivity that gets left behind when humanitarian institutions implement their particular forms of governance, but then pick up and move on without accounting for the remainders of their interventions.[13] Junaid himself mentioned that the UNHCR mission in Malaysia quickly preoccupied itself with the Rohingya refugees after its Aceh mandate ended.

Junaid clearly looks to the international humanitarian community for some kind of recognition, but his is a story of failure, including the story of our encounter. After a half hour of awkward misunderstandings and repetitions, when Junaid finally realized I had nothing to offer, he wished me a safe trip back to Banda Aceh, and took his leave. Since our meeting was unexpected and off topic from the goals of my journey, I might have even forgotten about our encounter altogether if not for the interview's recording that reminded me something was amiss if I only relied upon the easier and more relatable stories that others like Sami had shared with me. But even with the recording, I could not make sense of our conversation until I had a chance to listen to it a few times, to sort through the ambiguous pronouns, the rhythm of looping repetitions, and the heavy accent peppered with vocabulary more typically spoken in Malaysia. This dialectic misunderstanding brushed against the planned narrative of my reunion tour with old friends, inserting another truth about Aceh's humanitarian encounter into the story.

I introduce people like Dona and Junaid as unrecognized, ambivalent figures who populate the outskirts of Aceh's post-conflict landscape as a way to challenge and interrupt what might otherwise have been overly neat and coherent narratives of Aceh's recovery from tsunami and war.[14] This is an explicit nod to Mary's influence on my research. Figures on the outskirts offer "unofficial narratives" once we learn how to include them in our reading practice. In her earlier work, Mary defines an "unofficial narrative" as partial in both senses of the word: "explicitly partisan, interested accounts," on the one hand, incomplete and fragmentary on the other, "hence their fundamental indeterminacy."[15] On the outskirts of some tentative ideas I developed about humanitarian recognition and restoration of national subjectivity in post-conflict

---

[12] Grayman, "Official and Unrecognized Narratives of Recovery." For more on Aceh's diaspora and the conflict-era experiences that they carry into the present, see: Antje Missbach, *Separatist Conflict in Indonesia: The Long-Distance Politics of the Acehnese Diaspora* (London: Taylor & Francis, 2011).

[13] See: Mariella Pandolfi, "Contract of Mutual (In)Difference: Governance and the Humanitarian Apparatus in Contemporary Albania and Kosovo," *Indiana Journal of Global Legal Studies* 10, 1 (2003): 369–81; and Byron J. Good, Jesse Hession Grayman, and Mary-Jo DelVecchio Good, "Humanitarianism and 'Mobile Sovereignty' in Strong State Settings: Reflections on Medical Humanitarianism in Aceh, Indonesia," in *Medical Humanitarianism: Ethnographies of Practice*, ed. Sharon Abramowitz and Catherine Panter-Brick (Philadelphia: University of Pennsylvania Press, 2015), 155–75.

[14] Grayman, "Official and Unrecognized Narratives of Recovery," 550.

[15] Mary Margaret Steedly, *Hanging without a Rope: Narrative Experience in Colonial and Postcolonial Karoland* (Princeton: Princeton University Press, 1993), 135.

Aceh, these unofficial, Mary-esque stories resist easy interpretation and insert a productive and necessary tension into Aceh's taken-for-granted narratives of recovery.

SPIRITS

Manduhai Buyandelger

Spirits and mediums have a special place in Mary Steedly's work. Regrettably, I never inquired as to why she became interested in studying them. Our conversations always began from the middle of something—an encounter in the field, or a story, or a concept that needed to be unpacked. The demands of the present always seemed more urgent than the past, so we never reached the beginning of our shared interest in spirits.

Yet today I wonder how spirits might have contributed to Mary's highly original and at times unexpected way of seeing and thinking. I seek an answer to this question by rereading her work. In her first book, *Hanging without a Rope*, on narrative experience and spirits during the postcolonial period, and in her later writing on popular supernaturalism during the *Reformasi* period, Mary steers us toward the significance of spirits and the supernatural as providers of an unusual kind of light on things that we often take for granted.[1]

> Stories of spirits, situated outside the ordinary routines of social life yet with profound everyday effects, make visible the transparent conventions of narrative performance and of ethnographic evidence. In the circumscribed arenas of ritual enactment or on the wild borderlands of a familiar social world, encounters with spirits confront official standards of plausibility and good sense; truth here must come to terms with strangeness, strangeness with the regulative disciplines of narration.[2]

Manduhai Buyandelger is an associate professor at the Massachusetts Institute of Technology.

[1] See: Mary Margaret Steedly, *Hanging without a Rope: Narrative Experience in Colonial and Postcolonial Karoland* (Princeton: Princeton University Press, 1993); and Mary Margaret Steedly, "Transparency and Apparition: Media Ghosts of Post-New Order Indonesia," in *Images That Move,* ed. Patricia Spyer and Mary Margaret Steedly (Sante Fe: School for Advanced Research Press, 2013), 257–94.

[2] Steedly, *Hanging without a Rope*, 15.

In *Hanging without a Rope*, Mary weaves the stories of encounters with spirits and mediums—her stories and those of others—into an intricate matrix, thus revealing a space of a particular narrative experience. Each encounter pushes someone out of a comfort zone, destabilizing a recognized identity, revealing the fragility of a boundary ("border between two worlds"), or undermining confidence in one's understanding of something at hand. Whether in the ritual world of Karo mediumship or in the "lush mediascape" of popular Indonesian supernaturalism, the more we try to look at the supernatural, the more fragmentary and inconclusive it appears.[3]

While these two projects (one on spirit mediums and the other on technologically mediated images of spirit) are different and separated by twenty years, they complement each other. Attention to the supernatural offers Mary an unusual lens on the twists and turns of Indonesia's historical transformation from a modernizing postcolonial nation to the mass media-saturated, post-New Order era.

When Mary encountered spirit mediums in the 1980s, the postcolonial government had reduced spirits and their mediums (and also bandits) to a "simple representation of the disorder and danger" that it obviously intended to suppress.[4] Not only the spirits and mediums, but also many Karo people felt that they were left out of modernization; they were suspended, unable to move either forward or backward. Mary sheds light on flexible social relations, as opposed to official spaces, within which the spirits and mediums were incorporated. It is in this unofficial space that much of *Hanging without A Rope* takes place.[5]

Hanging without a Rope is a bustling space where mediums, especially female ones, could speak as someone else and thus convene an audience, which was nearly impossible when women stayed within the confines of their socially prescribed gender identities. Was the medium's ability to speak as someone else an appeal of the spirit world?

Don't be too excited, warns Mary. Performing *seluk* (a Karo term for a spirit possession) is neither women's empowerment nor a resistance to male hegemonic authority. *Seluk* is "a mobile and untranslatable subversion of identity."[6] When women speak through plural voices, there is a chance to escape from the language of subjects and objects, albeit only temporarily. Although "nowhere in the world are women silent," women's stories often do not fit the established Aristotelian narrative canon with logical sequences and satisfying endings for the public arena.[7] "Shaped to long acquaintances rather than transient encounter," women tell stories not in public, but while being constantly interrupted by the inevitable duties of the caretakers of small children and the elderly, while cooking and tending to all urgent matters of life.[8] Their

---

[3] Steedly, "Transparency and Apparition," 266.

[4] Steedly, *Hanging without a Rope*, 125.

[5] Although, as noted above, Mary returned to the theme of spirits in her later work, in what follows I focus on her earlier work, which influenced me the most.

[6] Steedly, *Hanging without a Rope*, 197.

[7] Steedly, *Hanging without a Rope*, 198.

[8] Steedly, *Hanging without a Rope*, 180.

stories get interrupted, shift around, start in the middle, repeat with a different emphasis, and often remain inconclusive.[9]

For this reason, Mary argues, it is necessary to expand our listening practices to include the "narrative shreds" beyond those stories with familiar structures. The problem of women's narratives is not in women or in women's speech. The problem is in the listeners or lack of listening and a lack of listening to the diversity of speech. Indeed, Mary explains, a spirit medium, after all, is not a different person even when she lends her voice to the spirits. Conventionally, it is believed that spirits displace the mediums' consciousness. But "privately," Mary writes, mediums "describe the experience in terms closer to the interhabitational ambiguity of *seluk*: as a kind of doubled vision, a semidetached awareness at once their own and that of another. Ask a medium directly and she will deny any knowledge of her trance experiences; yet memories of *seluk* are regularly cited in mediums' conversations … conversely, a spirit may ambiguously identify itself with the experiences and feelings of its human 'perch.'" Mary calls this experience a "double-determined speech."[10] The mediums do not see this as a sign of their weakness, but as the inconstancy of the spirits' presence (to which I will return later on). The audiences, however, tend to seek monologic singular messages, and often choose to ignore the multiplicity of voices in the mediums' speech.

Mary contrasts the mediums' double-determined speech with the Western notion of autonomous subjects, whose words, ideas, and voices are treated as the "'private property' of individual consciousness."[11] She suggests that a narrative production, which involves appropriating words from another context, is a kind of "discursive possession" that is also temporary and partial. The multiplicity, ambiguity, and inconstancy of the spirits further destabilize the narratives. Indeed, who borrows the mediums' speech? There are spirits that get merged with other spirits, there are split spirits, foreign spirits with or without their own translators, imposter spirits, doubles of the famous spirits, and spirits made of fragments of the dead to deploy for evil purposes.

Skilled mediums inhabit multiple identities, and there is a blurred identification of medium and spirit. We learn about the mediums' experiences of being someone else through their narrative performance. "We cannot simply step into other lives, fictional or not," Mary says. But "they can offer some insight into the processes by which experience is narratively produced and enmeshed in the practices of everyday discourse."[12]

Ephemeral, unseen, often ambivalent in their suggestions (because of their own decontextualized existence during possession), incoherent, and free from expectations and responsibilities of the current political era, they push the limits of the certainty of ethnographic knowledge and coherence of established narratives.

---

[9] Steedly, *Hanging without a Rope*, 108.
[10] Steedly, *Hanging without a Rope*, 196, 197.
[11] Steedly, *Hanging without a Rope*, 200.
[12] Steedly, *Hanging without a Rope*, 24.

Therefore, for Mary, spirits were also one of her conceptual lenses by which to take an alternative path, to consider misfits and to consider a variety of narrative experiences. Mary was committed to telling stories situated "on the edge of exclusion, on the borderlands of narrative plausibility—though not, for that reason, outside of ideology."[13]

When I was just beginning my research on Mongolian shamanism, I mentioned to her that the women I met tended to recoil from my questions. They befriended me, but when it came to questions about their shamanic experiences, they sent me to their male counterparts—their husbands, fathers, or teachers—who were very excited to converse with me about their worldviews and the meaning of their craft. "Oh, what a surprise," Mary laughed. Our conversation centered on talking to women and paying attention to those who were hiding or being quiet. From that day on, I shifted my attention to "misfits," the marginalized and misrecognized, both in human and spirits worlds.

What did this shift in my perspective reveal in considering the experiences and perspectives of misfits among newly reviving shamanic practitioners in post-socialist Mongolia? It was the 1990s, a period of a rapid transformation from state socialism to neoliberal capitalism, when previously suppressed shamanic practices were gaining prominence, but with much contention about the authenticity of spirits and the credibility of shamans who had to start from a generational gap in shamanic knowledge. Some spirits performed the stereotypes of their times, and were brimming with identities and powers. They belonged mostly to male shamans, because they had resources and labor to tend to the spirits. However, the incomplete spirits with partial identities, struggling to reach their destinations, and lacking voices and power to influence, and even to appear in rituals, were mostly attached to female shamans who were struggling economically and personally, and thus, living discreetly.

The spirits' power was directly related to the influence of their descendants, thus the present shaping the past and not the other way around. In my book, *Tragic Spirits*, I show this with the stories of two different female shamans, both of whom were considered equally powerful during socialist state suppression.[14] Yet, one had a son who became a famous shaman after socialism, and her many male and female students further expanded the prominence of that female spirit. Well-recognized, they even traveled to Italy and France, visiting Catholic temples and appeasing pagan spirits. The second shaman (who was equally powerful during her lifetime) had a daughter, Tuya, and a son. Tuya was ill and poor. The shaman's son was an atheist, and renounced his shaman mother while she was still alive, which was seen as the main reason behind the misfortunes of the second shaman's descendants. The spirit of this shaman was barely remembered among her immediate circles in the local community, while mythical stories about her circulated in the distance.

While spending time with Tuya, the daughter of this second shaman during my fieldwork, I listened to the narrative shreds that she had hardly ever articulated before. I recognized the patterns of narratives that Mary discusses. Situated on the edge of exclusion, they had multiple plots. The incomplete stories were repeated with different

---

[13] Steedly, *Hanging without a Rope*, 31.

[14] Manduhai Buyandelger, *Tragic Spirits: Gender, Memory, and Violence in Contemporary Mongolia* (Chicago: University of Chicago Press, 2013).

emphases depending on the intention of the speaker. The shaman's daughter was experiencing a "discursive possession" of a special kind. Influenced by her mother, but also by her own daughter, who had been initiated as a shaman, Tuya was sandwiched between two generations of shamans, the socialist shaman mother and postsocialist healer daughter. Years after I wrote *Tragic Spirits* and after I reread *Hanging without a Rope* once again for the purpose of writing this memorial piece, I realized that Tuya's mediation was a way of being someone else. She did so by mediating between the two opposing political systems, and two loving generations, thus creating a narrative of plausibility and continuity, albeit to a limited extent.

Indeed, in *Hanging without a Rope*, Mary discusses at least four ways of recognizing a possibility of other kinds of experience, or fleeting moments of being someone else. These are narrative experiences of different kinds. Mediumship is one way of recognizing others' experiences. Being a reader or a listener is a second way of attending to someone else's stories and extending one's personal understanding of another's experience. The third is being an ethnographer, especially during dramatic incidents during your fieldwork when you realize various shifts in your moral or political commitments. And fourth, being a writer, or constructing a narrative about other people's lives and stories. Tuya's fragmentary storytelling was akin to the last.

These four engagements—being a medium, a listener or reader, an ethnographer, and a writer—are all based on a voluntary displacement, a mobility of one's identity, and being a subject of one's own narration while also being shaped by others' narratives as well. Together they lead to a suspension from a unitary or prescribed identity to apprehend others' experiences. Mary helps us to remember that we are all a multitude of identities, which gives us an opportunity to take a step back from labeling, categorizing, and even interpreting others.

Spirits do much more than trouble our identities and subjectivities. The spirit world is eerie not only because of the invisible powers associated with it, but also because of its effect on the living, and the light that it shines on the presumed comfort zones and seeming realness of our own worlds, including the nature of ethnographic plausibility. It is eerie because spirits address the very uncertainties and difficulties that we hide from ourselves, thus disrupting the daily flow of what we are, and helping us to recognize our own doubleness.

Haunting

Byron J. Good and Mary-Jo DelVecchio Good

> Traces of violence are etched with microscopic intricacy into the
> experience of daily life … Narrative experience is not a free zone
> of imaginative resistance, but the space where political
> subjects come to recognize themselves. This does
> not mean that there is no possibility of liberation.
> I have, then, one last story to tell you here …
>
> —Mary Margaret Steedly

So begins the story of Setia Aron Ginting, former top cadre of the Communist party in Karoland, North Sumatra, who disappeared in the immediate post-Gestapu period and whose spirit was called home for the first—and last—time in 1985, as told by Mary Steedly in the last chapter of *Hanging without a Rope*.[1] Nandé Rita, his wife, had decided to become a Christian, and after her baptism there would be no chance to lay his unquiet spirit to rest. He had disappeared suddenly, presumably executed, Mary tells us, and had gone unmemorialized and largely unmourned, except by his wife and children in private. "Dead or alive," she writes, "he had been a danger to all those who knew him. And indeed he still was."[2] Yet by 1985, Nandé Rita felt it was time to call him back, learn the details of his death, perform the ceremonies of separation, and "lay his violent soul to rest." And so a séance was arranged—one like many Mary had

---

Byron J. Good is a professor of medical anthropology and Mary-Jo DelVecchio Good is a professor of global health and social medicine, both at Harvard University.

[1] Mary Margaret Steedly, *Hanging without a Rope: Narrative Experience in Colonial and Postcolonial Karoland* (Princeton: Princeton University Press, 1993), 224–40 (epigraph from 227). "Gestapu" is the acronym for *Gerakan September Tigapuluh*, the Indonesian expression for the Thirtieth of September Movement.

[2] Steedly, *Hanging without a Rope*, 228.

observed, but in this case a séance that attracted an unusually large crowd to witness the descent of the spirit of a man with such a history. Would he return as an angry ghost, seeking revenge, some wondered?

The writings of Mary Steedly, our close friend and colleague for many years, are filled with stories of human engagements with spirits—in Karoland during the core years of New Order developmental ideology and politics, as well as in Indonesian horror films in the post-Suharto *Reformasi* years. We thus proposed to the editors of this collection to place Mary's writing in conversation with that of Derrida and others using the keyword "haunting." It was interesting, then, to return to *Hanging without a Rope* and to her essay on "media ghosts"[3] to examine anew how she engaged issues of "spectrality."[4] What is most striking on first reading is the near total absence of the term "haunting." There are the *keramat* of Mount Sibayak, fearful to some, wondrous helpers of others. There are the spirits of the dead, with those who died unnaturally most powerful and threatening, but at the same time strong protectors if tended properly. But "haunting" is not described as part of narrative experience in Mary's analyses.

The same is true, perhaps more surprisingly, in Mary's analysis of post-New Order horror films. Here we are in a world of *kuntilanak*, evil female spirits, and of *pocong*, those ghosts/corpses covered in white shrouds that have remained "tied" at burial so that the spirits remain captured and float about threateningly. Although frightening, these figures are part of the everyday world, certainly in Java where we ourselves work:

> Indonesians go to see horror films to see their own ghosts, which are frightening in very particular—one might say, familiar—ways. The ghosts in these films are resolutely local ... predicated on belief rather than disbelief.[5]

Mary quickly dispenses with the notion that these are about spirit "beliefs" in ontological terms, as she does also in *Hanging without a Rope*. "For most Indonesians, the problem of spirits is not an ontological one but rather a moral one: not whether spirits exist, but what to do with them."[6] The word "haunting" appears occasionally, as in *The Haunted House in Pondok Indah*,[7] and although the concept translates almost perfectly into Indonesian—*hantu* is a generic ghost or specter, *menghantui* is to haunt,

---

[3] Mary Margaret Steedly, "Transparency and Apparition: Media Ghosts of Post-New Order Indonesia," in *Images That Move*, ed. Patricia Spyer and Mary Margaret Steedly (Sante Fe: School for Advanced Research Press, 2013), 257–94.

[4] The best collection of cultural-studies essays on spectralities is Maria Del Pilar Blanco and Esther Peeren, eds., *The Spectralities Reader: Ghosts and Haunting in Contemporary Cultural Theory* (New York: Bloomsbury, 2013). Throughout writing this essay, we have ourselves engaged in a conversation between Mary's writings and our recent essays in last year's special issue of *Ethos* on Hauntology in Psychological Anthropology, edited by Byron J. Good and Sadeq Rahimi; see: Byron J. Good, "Hauntology: Theorizing the Spectral in Psychological Anthropology," and Mary-Jo DelVecchio Good, "Spectral Presences of Si Pai: Begoña Aretxaga's *Cipayo* and Uncanny Experiences of Si Pai in Aceh 2008," *Ethos* 47, 4 (December 2019): 411–26 and 480–88, respectively.

[5] Steedly, "Transparency and Apparition," 279, 280.

[6] Steedly, "Transparency and Apparition," 262.

[7] *Rumah Pondok Indah* [The Haunted House in Pondok Indah]; produced by Ravi Pridhnani and directed by Dede Ferdinand; released on September 12, 2013, by Studio Sembilan. Mary mentions this film as one of a number of popular horror films in "Transparency and Apparition," 262.

dihantui is to be haunted[8]—it is not part of Steedly's analysis of horror films. Instead, she takes up analysis in terms of visibility and invisibility, or, more specifically, transparency and apparition.

The essay "Transparency and Apparition" juxtaposes what Mary calls two of the post-New Order's "discursive keywords": *transparansi* (transparency) in the domain of politics and *penampakan* (apparition) in the realm of the supernatural. What links these two terms is the wish for something obscure or unseen to *make an appearance*."[9] *Transparansi* was an explicit demand of *Reformasi* activists, with the language of financial reform extended to wider domains of corruption, terror, and the "mystifying opacity of public events."[10] Here Steedly builds on Karen Strassler's discussion of "transparency" and the interplay of the invisible and visible, as it unfolded during efforts by activists to bring to light the cases of rape of Chinese women during the 1998 uprising.[11] Steedly brings this analysis instead to "the rampant proliferation of media genres devoted to the supernatural,"[12] carrying her to her second keyword, *penampakan*.

It is here that Mary makes a particularly astute move by translating the word *penampakan*—a term that means, literally, "appearance" (from *tampak*, "to appear or become visible")—as "apparition." In this she follows the biographer of Leo Lumanto, a celebrity psychic, in arguing that *penampakan* is used popularly to mean "the manifestation of ghosts or spirits in visible or apprehensible form."[13] Her essay leads us through the remarkable role of horror films in the rise and popularization of cinema in Indonesia, the flourishing of such films in the decade following Suharto's fall, and sources of their popularity. On one hand, they emerged in the *Reformasi* era as one of the sites of exuberant artistic and media expression and consumption, circulating via the internet and inexpensive CDs (legal and illegal), representing a new media freedom and configuring a world largely absent of adult authority figures and religiously neutral.[14] It is in this everyday world that threatening spirits, normally hidden from view, make their appearance. But Steedly goes on to make a more provocative argument about their popularity. A decade after the fall of Suharto, Mary wrote:

> today's youth endeavor to come to terms with a suppressed national past that can no longer remain buried nor entirely come to light; with consumerism as an end in itself and religion a source of violence and social fragmentation; and [with] the absence of a powerful central figure ..."[15]

---

[8] See Good, "Hauntology," for discussion.

[9] Steedly, "Transparency and Apparition," 261.

[10] Steedly, "Transparency and Apparition," 265.

[11] Karen Strassler, "Gendered Visibilities and the Dream of Transparency: The Chinese-Indonesian Rape Debate in Post-Suharto Indonesia," *Gender & History* 16, 3 (2004): 689–725. See also: Patricia Spyer, "Fire without Smoke and Other Phantoms of Ambon's Violence: Media Effects, Agency, and the Work of Imagination," *Indonesia* 74 (October 2002): 21–36; and James T. Siegel, "Early Thoughts on the Violence of May 13 and 14 in Jakarta," *Indonesia* 66 (October 1999): 75–108.

[12] Steedly, "Transparency and Apparition," 266.

[13] Steedly, "Transparency and Apparition," 266.

[14] Which is in contrast to New Order horror films; see Steedly, "Transparency and Apparition," 278.

[15] Steedly, "Transparency and Apparition," 268.

It is precisely in this social and political moment that horror films took on a new life, "offending in so many ways the virtues of bourgeois respectability, religious morality, and secular rationalism…." In this "market driven excursion in low taste," the "dream of transparent visibility intersects with the nightmare of apparition," constituting one of the "key sites of political *and* poetic world-making for this post-*Reformasi* generation."[16]

It is in the context of a suppressed national history that the ghosts of the New Order find a presence among the *pocong* and *kuntilanak* of the horror films. But why now, Mary asks.[17] Perhaps, an Indonesian journalist suggests, in a period of crisis, supernatural stories may seem more credible than news reporting. But Mary argues something more is at stake, quoting film director Joko Anwar: "It is probably because there are so many unexplained deaths in this country over such a long period of time that makes our local audiences interested in stories about ghosts who seek revenge from those who have wronged them," he wrote in 2002.[18] This association of revenge with the unexplained and unmourned dead remains present until today in talk about the dangers of genuinely revisiting past violence in Indonesian history; of, as Mary wrote, "the tentative efforts to disinter, both literally and figuratively, some of the New Order's victims."[19] It is this association that begins to point back to Mary's experiences of ghosts and questions of vengefulness decades earlier in her Karo work.

Thus we return not only to Karoland but to the final story Mary tells in *Hanging without a Rope*, the story of the séance to call Setia Aron Ginting back for a final visit with his wife and family. It is only here, in the final chapter of that book, that "haunting" makes an appearance as a critical analytic term. There was particular excitement in the village surrounding this séance because at the moment of return the spirit reenacts the moment of death. No one knew how Setia Aron had died—and even the question of whether he had died, had been imprisoned, or had gone into hiding remained open these many years later. In addition, many wondered if he would return as a vengeful spirit. "Now we will find out how he really died," a friend told Mary. "And what will he say then to all of you good people who've come to watch him die again?" another friend asked rhetorically, and concluded, mimicking Setia Aron's imagined words, "I'll kill you all!"[20]

Mary takes us in detail through Nandé Pajuh's séance, culminating in the appearance of Setia Aron's spirit at about midnight. And thus Nandé Rita could finally learn how her husband had died. "His hands were pulled behind his back as if they were tied; his legs stretched out in front of him. His body twitched several times as if struck by bullets. The death was a slow, gradual one. The onlookers wept."[21] The spirit spoke briefly about his death—where he had been taken off the bus, how he had been taken to a riverbank infamous as the site of executions. There he was shot. But instead of scolding those who had failed to conduct his funeral—"No one would have dared to

---

[16] Steedly, "Transparency and Apparition," 270.

[17] Steedly, "Transparency and Apparition," 280.

[18] Quoted in Steedly, "Transparency and Apparition," 280.

[19] Steedly, "Transparency and Apparition," 280.

[20] Steedly, *Hanging without a Rope*, 230.

[21] Steedly, *Hanging without a Rope*, 234.

come! Who would have dared to be seen at his funeral?"[22]—Setia Aron began instead to sing in the conventional style of funeral mourners."

> Arms flung wide, bowing deeply in time to the song's rhythm, he continued to sing, telling of the hardships Nandé Rita had undergone and how he had longed to see her again, of her diligence in raising their children through difficult times. Nandé Rita sat quietly with downcast eyes, weeping.[23]

He called his children, charged his son to take his place. He called his sisters and father's sisters, scolding them for not attending to Nandé Rita. He told how he had lost his way, become caught up in their [the Communist party's] activities, accepted responsibility. And he told all present that he had protected his family "by erasing the history of his life and his death from public memory,"[24] enabling them all to move on with their lives. At 3:00 AM, he departed.

> Setia Aron's absence would henceforth be his memorial, for he had appropriated the silence that surrounded him, and offered it to his family as a parting gift, a sign of his power.[25]

It is only here, at the end of this final story, that Mary evokes haunting:

> Many more than those who killed and those who were their victims have become entrapped in the frozen moment of mass violence that inaugurated Indonesia's New Order. Every effort to erase this bloody haunting further saturates its environment with the fear and horror that are its lingering traces … These local agonies are seeded and cultivated in national memory, ensuring that they, like the deaths of a single day, will never end.[26]

Setia Aron's return responds to the "monologic versions of the past," but not with a "counter-official" history. Mary Steedly suggests that, rather than searching for these, we attend to "the stories of personal experience that emerge discordantly from the orderly flow of generic representations to suggest other, partial realities, other mappings of the social terrain."[27] She continues:

> Setia Aron's voice, called back from an uncertain death, moves across these images [of the spectral Communist enemy] to reveal a singular life and death, one still deeply entangled in the social web of others' lives. Setia Aron returns not with threats to "kill you all," … but with a word for the other victims of the reprisals…"[28]

He speaks to his mother who lost her son, to his children who have lived in the shadow of his life and death, but most of all to Nandé Rita. Mary concludes her book:

---

[22] Steedly, *Hanging without a Rope*, 229.
[23] Steedly, *Hanging without a Rope*, 235.
[24] Steedly, *Hanging without a Rope*, 236.
[25] Steedly, *Hanging without a Rope*, 236.
[26] Steedly, *Hanging without a Rope*, 237.
[27] Steedly, *Hanging without a Rope*, 238.
[28] Steedly, *Hanging without a Rope*, 239.

For them, and all the others left hanging without a rope in the New Order's Age of Development, remembrance is still shadowed by fear, but forgetfulness is no remedy. The souls of the dead still haunt the banks of the blood-red rivers; unmourned and unpropitiated, they return silently to plague those who, out of fear or out of faith, have failed to acknowledge them.[29]

Mary did not engage theories of haunting explicitly. But her powerful concluding chapter, along with her writing about "media ghosts" of the New Order,[30] suggest important directions for placing this work in conversation with recent writings on hauntology.[31] For Derrida, "learning to live with" spirits, ghosts, and phantoms, which leave their traces in language, require a hauntology, not a resort to ontology.[32] Avery Gordon describes haunting as "an animated state in which a repressed or unresolved social violence is making itself known, sometimes very directly, sometimes more obliquely … The whole essence … of a ghost is that it has real presence and demands its due."[33] What, we might ask, is the nature of haunting as *narrative experience*, and what can we know about the "subject" of such haunting? What would constitute a distinctive hauntology, perhaps a *hantuologi*, for contemporary Indonesia?[34] What is distinctive about Indonesian political ocularity, the way Aceh or Papua are simultaneously seen and not seen, the violence known and not known? A psychological anthropologist would want to put Mary's work in conversation with Freud's writing on the uncanny, something "secretly familiar which has undergone repression and returned from it," a special form of making visible that which should not be seen, and the terror that follows one seeing what one should not see.[35]

Why at certain moments in history do the ghosts of past violence make their insistent presence felt, often in myriad forms, Mary asks?[36] When are such appearances therapeutic, cathartic? And when do they provoke powerful repressive responses to the making visible of that which should have remained hidden? What does it mean to say that Indonesia is haunted, even today, by the events of 1965–66, or by the

---

[29] Steedly, *Hanging without a Rope*, 240.

[30] Steedly's writing about "media ghosts" involved a single essay, which leaves us wishing for more. We are left with a sense of Steedly's related ideas being unfinished, though she nevertheless moved on in her writing.

[31] See Good, "Hauntology."

[32] Jacques Derrida, *Specters of Marx: The State of the Debt, the Work of Mourning, and the New International* (New York: Routledge, 1994). This book is translated into Indonesian as *Hantu Hantu Marx: Keadaan Utang, Karya Belasungkawa, & Internasional Baru* (Yogyakarta: Narasi-Pustaka Promothea, 2015).

[33] Avery Gordon, *Ghostly Matters: Haunting and the Sociological Imagination*, second edition (Minneapolis: University of Minnesota Press, 2008), xvi.

[34] For a fuller discussion, see Good, "Hauntology."

[35] Sigmund Freud, *The Uncanny* (New York: Penguin, 1919, 2003). Freud's analysis turns on the tale of the Sand Man, who throws sand in the eyes of naughty children, "so that their eyes jump out of their heads, all bleeding." It is this primitive terror, associated with ocularity and rooted in the unconscious, that produces the sense of the uncanny, Freud suggests.

[36] Kenneth George suggests that this dramatic appearance of apparitions was well underway toward the end of the New Order. It was during this time that "a convincing and thoroughgoing state-sponsored civility" gives birth to "a myriad of demonic fears and apparitions—ghosts, Draculas, and corpses endlessly threatening a cultured calm," warning of the end of an era; see Kenneth George, "Violence, Culture, and the Indonesian Public Sphere: Reworking the Geertzian Legacy," in *Violence: Culture, Performance, and Expression*, ed. Neil L. Whitehead (Santa Fe: School for Advanced Research Press, 2004): 27–28.

disappearances of students or the rapes of Chinese women? Or that the *kuntilanak* or *pocong* horror films, or the ninjas that appeared following Suharto's fall, represent ghosts of New Order violence?

Mary's analysis rejected any simple reductions, while keeping just such questions alive. And with her remarkable story about Setia Aron's spirit's visit, when he turned a potential moment of vengeance into a space for mourning, she raises the question about the capacity for healing the remainders of violence.

> I had come to Setia Aron's séance hoping to discover a form of disguised political resistance encoded in ritual … I was disappointed … when Nandé Pajuh, through her spirit helper Pathfinder, insisted that politics should have no place in the séance. Her insight was of course keener than mine; and I later saw that by so restricting the scene of Setia Aron's return Nandé Pajuh created the possibility for a more profound subversion and the hope of a mutual healing. Bypassing the official language of blame and betrayal, she could open up a loophole in history, creating, for a moment, an unofficial elsewhere beyond the truths of Old and New Orders, where families and neighbors could begin again to converse with one another in the proper Karo manner, as kin.[37]

---

[37] Steedly, *Hanging without a Rope*, 237–38.

Memory

Karen Strassler

To read Mary Steedly's *Hanging without a Rope* and *Rifle Reports* is to enter an atmosphere saturated with pasts that refuse to stay still.[1] "Memory" in Mary's hands is always a mercurial substance: it shifts and slides, sometimes gathering into discernable forms and other times trickling off into shimmering rivulets that go nowhere. Some elements spin out into discrete, scattered droplets, never to rejoin the dominant stream. Memories may momentarily conform to the molds provided by available genres and shared narrative scripts, but they never commit finally to those shapes, they continually overflow their containers, leak or burst out, take on new forms.

In *Hanging without a Rope* and *Rifle Reports*, Karo Batak practices of remembering follow meandering paths that neither lead to neat conclusions nor follow clear arcs; they remain fragmentary and open to uncertain futures. The recollections in these texts yield an intricate tracery spun around the negative spaces of silences and gaps, of stories untold and violence unassimilated. A motley accumulation of irreverent jokes; sentimental song; snippets of dialogue; ghostly apparitions; mundane lists of places and tasks; and sensuous recollections of tastes, smells, and dirt on the hands builds up a "thicket" of memory that is ambiguous, resonant, unruly.[2] Rather than impose coherence, Mary's accounts mimetically conjure how life is lived and recalled: as a palimpsest of only partially and provisionally successful attempts to give shape to—or communicate to others—what has been felt and known, seen and heard.

Karen Strassler is an associate professor in the department of anthropology at Queens College and the Graduate Center of City University of New York. She thanks the participants of "The Said and the Unsaid: Honoring the Legacy of Mary Margaret Steedly" roundtable at the American Anthropological Association Meetings in San Jose, California, in November 2018, and she especially thanks Smita Lahiri and Patricia Spyer for their comments on earlier drafts of this essay.

[1] Mary Margaret Steedly, *Hanging without a Rope: Narrative Experience in Colonial and Postcolonial Karoland* (Princeton: Princeton University Press, 1993); and Mary Margaret Steedly, *Rifle Reports: A Story of Indonesian Independence* (Berkeley: University of California Press, 2013).

[2] Steedly, *Hanging without a Rope*, 15.

Memories—those "densely layered, sometimes conflictual negotiations with the passage of time"—do not serve to "complete" or "set straight" a historical record.[3] Mary was not trying to locate authentic, oppositional voices or to excavate evidence by which to contest official historical accounts. She refused a naïve and instrumentalist approach to memory as a source of subaltern truths to be tapped. She argued that events are never received as naked happenings, never spared what she called the "transformative energies of storytelling."[4] Experiences are always already dressed in narratives that anticipate and prefigure them, cast through and against iconic figures and dominant tropes, and reworked in dialogue with other stories and subsequent occurrences. Memories have specific tellers and tellings, but—in a Bakhtinian sense—they never belong, finally, to a single speaker or moment. What matters, then, is "not what really happened ... but rather why [something came] to be recalled and retold in one particular way and not another ... and what might be at stake" in that particular time and manner of telling.[5]

What always strikes me when reading Mary's ethnographic work is her deep affection and respect for the people she writes about, her sensitivity to their artfulness, her refusal to reduce them and their stories to social positions and types, and her resistance (not only in her writing!) to all forms of solemnization or aggrandizement. She conveyed the often obscure (for a non-Karo reader) poetics of Karo accounts, offering an intimate sense of a people to those of us with no other access to them. Mary's work foregrounded "popular memory": recollections of extraordinary events by ordinary people that tended to be organized around tropes of irony and ignorance more than moral virtue and sacrifice, around mundane objects and routines as much as heroic exploits, around a sense of the past registered as inchoate sensation and longing rather than formulated ideological commitment. In both form and content, popular memory accounts punch irreverent holes in the sacral myths of official nationalism, though they can never be neatly placed outside of them.

I am only beginning to fully recognize the profound impact of Mary's work on my own. My first research in Indonesia began in 1996, when I was still a graduate student. I was working on an oral history project led by my advisor, Ann Laura Stoler, interviewing people who had worked as servants in Dutch households.[6] In asking about former servants' experiences at the close of the colonial era, we were probing into a past that existed on the margins of officially recognized, national "History." The people we interviewed were not practiced storytellers, their accounts had no audience, and they themselves did not imagine that their stories could matter. Their answers to our questions were "uncrafted, rough-hewn, and apparently unrehearsed," we wrote in a subsequent article, because their memories existed "outside the comfort zone" of official history.[7]

---

[3] Steedly, *Rifle Reports*, 268.

[4] Steedly, *Rifle Reports*, 265.

[5] Steedly, *Rifle Reports*, 308.

[6] Fellow graduate student Dias Pradadimara and, later, two researchers, Nita Kariani Purwanti and Didi Kwartanada, also worked on this project.

[7] Ann Laura Stoler and Karen Strassler, "Castings for the Colonial: Memory Work in 'New Order' Java," *Comparative Studies in Society and History* 42, 1 (January 2000): 4–48.

In that article, Ann and I cited Mary just once, acknowledging her account of the New Order regime's control of the past through the cultivation of fear.[8] Yet, in retrospect, I believe that *Hanging without a Rope* was my most important guide in that first foray into "ethnographic history."[9] More than anyone else, it was Mary who taught me to think critically about "subaltern" accounts of the past, who modeled for me how to listen for the unsaid and the too-often repeated. It was she who taught me not to expect coherence from the unscripted recollections of those whose memories had not been accorded value within official narratives. *Hanging without a Rope* demonstrated how to approach these memories with respect for their form, how to resist the temptation to tame and claim them.

It embarrasses me now that I did not see this then. But I think it is the nature of a book like *Hanging without a Rope*, which does not so much announce its theorizing as enact it, that it could thoroughly shape the way I approached both ethnographic practice and memory accounts, and yet leave me unaware of its influence. Mary's book worked on me. It became part of my very make-up as an anthropologist. Such debts elude the normal practices of academic citation.

I recall visiting Gadjah Mada University in 1996 to seek the counsel of Indonesian historians in my search for former servants of the Dutch. I remember their bafflement at my interest in this subject, and their attempts to reorient me to the more "important" aspects of colonial history. I recall, too, an impressive wall of bookcases full of cassette-tape recordings of oral histories of *pejuang* (revolutionary fighters). These were object lessons: the material artifacts of the legions of students, armed with tape recorders on a mission to preserve revolutionary history, whose journeys into urban *kampung* (neighborhoods) and rural *desa* (villages) made clear whose stories, and which pasts, counted. Yet in *Rifle Reports*, Mary stepped right into that over-trodden, over-determined, enshrined revolutionary past. With the irreverent and fragmentary stories of Karo women who had experienced the revolution from the outskirts, she put chaos, uncertainty, violence, and humor in the place where sanctity had been.

Rereading *Rifle Reports* after Mary's death, I was struck by the term "memory artist," which she used to describe Sinek, a singer whose recorded song about her harrowing experiences as an evacuee during the revolution Mary explored in depth in a published essay and then again in *Rifle Reports*.[10] The memory artist, Mary wrote, creates a "collective history" out of "singular testimony."[11] A figure of modernity, the memory artist emerges at precisely the moment that earlier ways of transmitting the past—myth and ritual, epic and custom—have lost their grip; she centers her narrative on individual biography and experiences of rupture rather than continuity. "[T]hose persons that I call 'memory artists,'" Mary wrote, drawing inspiration from Walter Benjamin's meditation on the storyteller, "transmute the materials of personal experiences into the story of a community … the memory artist renders the experience

---

[8] Stoler and Strassler, "Castings for the Colonial," 14.

[9] Mary Margaret Steedly, "Author's Response: Mary Margaret Steedly," in "Reviewed Work(s): *Rifle Reports: A Story of Indonesian Independence*, by Mary Margaret Steedly," in *Sojourn* 30, 3 (November 2015): 870.

[10] Mary Margaret Steedly, "Modernity and the Memory Artist," *Comparative Studies in Society and History* 42, 4 (October 2000): 811–46.

[11] Steedly, "Modernity and the Memory Artist," 814.

of loss in graspable, personal form, to a primary audience of those who were there too. The memory artist incites in her audience the desire to remember and gives them something to recall."[12]

Mary's conceptualization of the memory artist resonates for me now because of my own recent writing on a body of work by a Chinese Indonesian visual artist, FX Harsono.[13] Harsono's artworks address the chaotic and violent period of the revolution described in *Rifle Reports*, but from the vantage point of ethnic Chinese in Java. They bring into public view memories of massacres of ethnic Chinese at the hands of nationalist militias. Like Mary's memory artist, Harsono seeks an audience for stories excluded from the grand narratives of national history. In staging "public dramatizations of personal experience," Harsono's art provides "both pattern and stimuli for popular imagination" of a collective past.[14]

Unlike Sinek, Mary's exemplary memory artist, Harsono is not an immediate survivor of the violence (he was born shortly afterward and grew up in its shadow). In his series of works on the revolutionary-era massacres in Java, Harsono draws on an album of photographs taken by his father that were placed on a shelf in the family home, alongside their family albums. In 1951, Harsono's father, who owned a photography studio, was commissioned by a national ethnic Chinese organization (Chung Hua Tsung Hui, Central Chinese Association) to document the exhumation and reburial of 191 Chinese victims of a massacre that had taken place on the outskirts of Blitar three years earlier.

In paintings such as *Preserving Life, Terminating Life I* and *Preserving Life, Terminating Life II*, Harsono juxtaposes his own family photographs with images from the exhumation showing the unearthing of skeletal remains. The uniting of these photographs within the frame of the painting insists that they be read with and against each other, suggesting the spectral violence that haunts the banal ordinariness of everyday life and refiguring the predictable milestones of family life as quietly heroic attempts to persist and imagine a future in the face of threat. In other works in his series on the revolutionary-era massacres, Harsono draws on interviews with survivors, rubbings of graves, and mundane objects like radios, wheelchairs, and domestic altars at which ethnic Chinese Indonesians pray to the dead. These assembled materials allow him to make viscerally present a past that has thus far only been remembered in hushed and fragmented family stories, embodied rituals, and mute artifacts.

It is the convening of a public that defines the work of the memory artist for Mary. "By publicly telling her own personal history," the memory artist "opens the work of imagination as collective cultural practice."[15] Both Harsono and Sinek reframe personal memories of communal trauma in aesthetic media that draw attention and affective response. Sinek's primary audience, Mary tells us, was fellow survivors who lived their own versions of the experiences she narrated, whereas Harsono addresses

---

[12] Steedly, *Rifle Reports*, 283.

[13] Karen Strassler, "Zones of Refuge: Fugitive Memories of Violence in the Work of FX Harsono," *History of the Present* 8, 2 (Fall 2018): 177–208.

[14] Steedly, *Rifle Reports*, 279.

[15] Steedly, "Modernity and the Memory Artist," 815.

contemporary Indonesian and international art publics who may know little of the past his art recalls. Crucially, though, Sinek's song was recorded, and this gave it the potential to speak beyond her original audience. It could, after all, be found by an American anthropologist rummaging in a dusty music shop in Medan. Through its reproduction, Sinek's song extends out to an open-ended public, including the readers of Mary's book. Reframing his father's photographs for new audiences and new purposes, Harsono's work also depends on the possibilities for soliciting new publics that technologies of reproduction afford.

It occurred to me as I thought about it further that Harsono in some ways has more in common with Mary (who found Sinek's cassette in a dark, neglected corner of a shop) than he does with Sinek. Like Mary, Harsono is not a direct witness, but a collector and artful compiler of marginal stories and obscure artifacts. Harsono and Mary both draw on these discarded traces to probe the excessive violence of the Indonesian revolution. Sinek's song, recorded in the 1950s, in fact elides the violence inflicted by Indonesians on Indonesians; it is Mary who points us to the silences that Sinek, in her bid to include Karo Batak experiences within the national story of the revolution, imposed. Mary's account, like Harsono's artwork, is oriented to the present and the future as it makes a place—or at least exposes the lack of place—for disavowed scenes of violence within the nation's origin story.

These resonances between Harsono's and Mary's work on the Indonesian revolution prompted me to recognize Mary herself as a kind of memory artist. Always attentive to what she called the "social production of ephemerality," especially when it came to women's narratives, her acts of listening generated a profoundly political sounding of history, one that insisted on hearing the "traces, textures, and tones" of a past that might otherwise be registered ever so faintly and fleetingly.[16] Through writing, she turned her own acts of listening into a practice of making audible. Mary's accounts registered otherwise fragile memories as marks that might stay with us.

A couple of months before she died, I asked Mary about her unfinished book on the Citadel, the South Carolina military academy that was her childhood home and where her father worked as a teacher. Was it possible that the manuscript—or parts of it—could be published as is? Could any of her beloved students or colleagues prepare it for publication on her behalf? Her answer was a decisive "No."

Mary had an exacting ear and a precise vision. Those who enjoyed conversation with her or witnessed her extemporaneous comments at conferences and talks know what a lively mind and a quick wit she possessed. But she worked slowly, giving her writing time to take shape. She could not imagine putting that book out into the world before it had fully assumed its form, nor could she accept anyone else doing that work for her. For Sinek, for Harsono, for Mary—memory-work lies in the artful honing of stories, in their poetic crafting. It was a great sadness to her, and is a loss to all of us, that the book most shaped by her own personal memories remained unfinished, for perhaps it was here that Mary would most fully have come into her own as a memory artist.

---

[16] Steedly, *Hanging without a Rope*, 29; and Steedly, *Rifle Reports*, 34.

AFTER ALL:
IN PLACE OF AN AFTERWORD

Kenneth M. George

Owing to the ethnographic project that Kirin Narayan and I have been running in India, I had to miss the memorial gatherings held in honor of Mary Steedly in San Jose and at Harvard last year (2018). Mary has mattered so much to me. For over forty years, she was a friend to whom I could always turn; and for many of those years, she was a close colleague with whom I could always trade ideas and laughs, looks of puzzlement, or the sighs of exasperation that come with being in an academic department. You would understand, then, how touched I was when Patsy, Karen, and Smita asked me to write an "afterword" for this special issue of *Indonesia* dedicated to remembering Mary. I, of course, said yes. Yet I am finding it impossible to write one after all. When you get right down to it, do eulogies and tributes and tears really want an "afterword"? I don't think so. Eulogies and tears want to be mimicked. They want more. They yearn to hold and spread through an audience or a crowd, and reflect the "fierce wish" of the grieving (says Elias Canetti) to find oneness with each other in mourning, and to summon the deceased back into their lives.[1]

My story about Mary picks up about the same time as Jim Peacock's, elsewhere in this issue. It's different than his, of course, because it's mine; I lived it, and I keep living with it, too. Memories of Mary keep coming back to me, sometimes fading, sometimes sticking. So the story's unfinished and keeps changing, going this way and that with different retellings.

For now, let me begin this way ...

Kenneth M. George is a professor of anthropology at Australian National University's College of Asia and the Pacific.

[1] Elias Canetti, *Crowds and Power*, trans. Carol Stewart (New York: Seabury Press, 1978), 105.

• • •

Mary showed up in the UNC (University of North Carolina) Folklore Program in January 1977, just as US President Jimmy Carter was about to take the oath of office.[2] The mood around Chapel Hill was warm and upbeat, all smiles and a sense that the South had been welcomed home with Carter's election. Mary was taking a course on "folk narrative," and so was I, and after class we would talk about this and that over coffee and a smoke on the steps of Lenoir Hall. She was living on her own, west of Chapel Hill and Carrboro, in an old farmhouse. It was a small place. She was keeping a goat—I don't know why or for whom—and I remember vines growing into the kitchen through the window sashes and chinks in the walls. Mary didn't stay out there very long. To make ends meet she worked for a state agency on a hypertension project, interviewing folks across two or three counties, with the aim of finding social factors behind the differential prevalence of the disease and resulting mortality rates across white and African-American families. I remember her explaining the different ways folks talked about the disease, and so from the get-go Mary always seemed to be fascinated by everyday ideas and everyday talk about healing and illness in the North Carolina countryside. I think that is what brought her to taking a course on folk narrative. Indonesia wasn't in the picture at all that spring.

Mary moved into town in the summer of 1977 and set up house with the most affectionate border collie one could want to find. Mary named her Tessa. I was up near Luray, Virginia, spending two months working with Jeff Titon on what would become the "Powerhouse for God" project, recording conversion stories, testimonies, chanted sermons, altar calls, and gospel songs.[3] My compass at the time aligned with the Black Mountain poets Charles Olson and Ed Dorn; the journals *Alcheringa* and *Place* (both now long gone); narratology, ethnopoetics, and the ethnography of speaking; and the symbolic anthropology of Victor Turner, Barbara Babcock, and others. Like Mary, my committee included Jim Peacock, Terry Zug, and Daniel Patterson (as chair). Her own reading, as I recall it from late 1977, leaned toward work by Clifford Geertz, Roland Barthes, Georg Lukacs, Claude Lévi-Strauss, and the same group of symbolic anthropologists who figured so prominently in Jim's orbit and who were so widely read at the time.[4] We both loved Walker Percy and were rereading him. Mary was now a full-time graduate student, and she would have been reading work in medical anthropology by this point, and Jim's *Consciousness and Change* and his *Rites of*

---

[2] This was roughly a year after Indonesia began *Operasi Seroja* (Operation Lotus), its invasion and military occupation of East Timor.

[3] Jeff Todd Titon, *Powerhouse for God: Speech, Chant, and Song in an Appalachian Baptist Church* (Austin: University of Texas Press, 1988). See also: Ken George and Jeff Titon, "Dressed in the Armor of God," *Alcheringa: Ethnopoetics* 3, 2 (1977): 10–31; Ken George and Jeff Titon, "Testimonies." *Alcheringa: Ethnopoetics* 4, 1 (1978): 69–83; and Kenneth M. George, "'I Still Got It:' The Conversion Narrative of John C. Sherfey" (unpublished MA thesis, University of North Carolina at Chapel Hill, 1978).

[4] A galvanizing event at UNC in spring 1978 was the visit of Victor Turner, Mary Douglas, and Thomas O. Beidelman for a symposium on social anthropology to commemorate the founding of the UNC anthropology program under the influence of Bronislaw Malinowski. Mary and I had a good laugh at how Mary Douglas presided over the stage from a centrally placed armchair, and kept the two boys in their "marginal" place during symposium discussion with her more than a little patronizing remarks.

Modernization.⁵ Those two books, and Geertz's essays on Java and Bali in his *Interpretation of Cultures*, gave Mary her first ethnographic glimpses of Indonesia.⁶

Mary was always a voracious and discerning reader, and I think her capacity to read widely and well was behind the artful, writerly style that she cultivated over the years and that has made such an impression on us as we remember her in this special issue. Yet especially striking and meaningful for me, too, have been her ethnographic sensibilities. I will never forget her buoyant return from a weekend in Lumberton, North Carolina, in April 1978, where she had gone to meet the Lumbee healer, Vernon Cooper, who would be central to her master's thesis. She just bubbled over with stories about their meeting, going on about their time together:

> … and so then he says, "Do *you* know what ideology is?" And I say, "Well, I'm not so sure I do." And he looks at me and leans over and says, "Ideology is when you can look someone in the eyes and tell what's wrong with 'em. *That's* eye-deology, and I know how to *use* it."

Mary broke out giggling, "Isn't that great?" To this day, I still chuckle over Cooper's remark about ideological and eye-deological diagnosis, and put it on par with any description of ideology and false consciousness. Mary's receptivity to the quirky, the marginal, and the surprise utterance, to dissonant and unsettling remarks, was already there well before her fieldwork in Indonesia. She never said so, but I think her ethnographic sensibilities found support and further refinement when she collaborated with Ruel Tyson in his fieldwork in churches around the state. Tyson, I know, was interested in what he called "ethnographic judgment," and before all else that her writing puts on show—be it about Karo spirit mediums, Indonesian horror movies, or "culinary nationalism" and eating elephants—I marvel at Mary's ethnographic acuity and awareness, her capacity to conjure the feel and often contradictory forces animating social life.

Mary faced a choice in 1979. She had decided to take a doctorate in anthropology, and prospects for doing fieldwork in Indonesia were now key to her ambitions. Cornell offered her a full ticket: years of support at what was at that time the leading US university for the study of Indonesia, and perhaps Southeast Asia more broadly. James Boon, she mentioned, was eager to work with her; and I wonder if Thomas Kirsch was as well.⁷ My hunch is that had she gone to Cornell, she would have been drawn into working closely with James Siegel, Ben Anderson, and their students, too; or so her writing on Indonesia inclines me to believe. Virginia and North Carolina made offers, as I recollect; I don't remember if the University of Chicago was in the mix, or Berkeley for that matter. Michigan, meanwhile, awarded her a FLAS (Foreign Language and Area Studies) fellowship in support of her graduate studies on Indonesia. Mary

---

⁵ See: James Peacock, *Consciousness and Change: Symbolic Anthropology in Evolutionary Perspective* (New York: Wiley, 1975); and James Peacock, *Rites of Modernization* (Chicago: University of Chicago Press, 1968).

⁶ Clifford Geertz, *The Interpretation of Cultures: Selected Essays* (New York: Basic Books, 1973).

⁷ Boon had been one of Jim Peacock's students, and Kirsch had been Peacock's colleague at Princeton, and together with Jim had taught "symbolic anthropology" for a few years.

decided to pursue her doctorate at the University of Michigan, with its strength not just in Indonesian studies, but also in medical and cultural anthropology.[8]

She arrived in Ann Arbor at a moment of opportune flux. A good number of cultural anthropology faculty had gone away on leave, altering the intellectual and curricular dynamics of the program. Michael ("Mick") Taussig's first book, *The Devil and Commodity Fetishism*,[9] was in press and Taussig, Mary's advisor, had taken the reins of the proseminar in anthropological theory, in addition to offering courses on medical anthropology and shamanism. The University of Chicago's Bernard Cohn was in residence for the year and engaging students with his interest in combining history and anthropology. Christopher "Kit" Davis (-Roberts) had arrived and was enthralling people with her readings in critical theory. Sherry Ortner was running a cutting-edge course on gender and hierarchy. The bookshelves in Mary's apartment may have been the best measure (and witness) of the intensity with which she applied herself in her early years at Michigan. They filled rapidly with books by (and on) Althusser, Bakhtin, de Beauvoir, Benjamin, Foucault, Carlo Ginzburg, Lacan, Frederic Jameson, Marx, Michelle Rosaldo and Louise Lamphere, and Raymond Williams; scads of novels; and ever-spilling stacks of photocopied articles on Indonesia, the anthropology of religion and healing, and the anthropology of gender. An IBM Selectric typewriter hummed at her altar of work. The backing soundtrack included the Clash, the Ramones, Tom Petty and the Heartbreakers, and The Police.

It wouldn't have crossed my mind back then, but I think those early years in Ann Arbor were a time when Mary was already at work alertly crafting for herself an intellectual and writerly style. We each went off to Indonesia and started our fieldwork projects at more or less the same time, not long after the 1982 national elections and just a couple of months before the first total eclipse of the sun visible in Indonesia in several hundred years. We exchanged letters once or twice, just at the beginning of our respective work in Medan and Mambi, and we both confessed that settling into and switching between national and local languages made us dizzy ... *bikin pusing*. We saw each other again only after each of us had returned to Ann Arbor in early 1986.

There was nothing about the cultural anthropology job market in 1986–87 that would have pushed anyone to finish a dissertation quickly, the advent of desktop computers notwithstanding. There was broad despair about the lack of jobs, leading to rueful jokes about doctoral students contacting "The Equalizer," the hero of a popular US television series in the late '80s featuring a retired secret agent who tries to protect everyday people from getting a raw deal, and who could be counted on to rescue good-hearted people from desperate circumstances. ("Maybe the Equalizer could have a frank word with the search committee about the shortlist," someone quipped.) *Anthropology as Cultural Critique* and *Writing Culture* were famously unsettling disciplinary conversations and gatherings at this time, and marking certain kinds of

---

[8] I had begun my doctorate at the University of Michigan the year before, unsure as to whether I would aim to specialize on Polynesia or on Indonesia and Southeast Asia more broadly. It was Mary who suggested—in a phone call, or was it in a letter?—that I look into the Sa'dan Toraja highlands of Sulawesi. I should add here, too, that the University of Michigan happened to be where Mary's father took his degree—in chemistry, if I am not wrong. Mary was born in Ann Arbor in 1946, and spent some of her infancy there.

[9] Michael T. Taussig, *The Devil and Commodity Fetishism in South America* (Chapel Hill: University of North Carolina Press, 1980).

fault lines among and between reading formations.[10] Mary read these two works, to be sure, but I believe far more key to her sensibilities was her immersion into her Karo fieldnotes and into colonial era accounts and reports on the Karo region.[11] This was in keeping with her pursuit of historical ethnography.[12] Meanwhile, Cornell's Ben Anderson had published his magisterial *Imagined Communities* while we were in the field,[13] and that had an immense impact on her thinking as she began to craft her dissertation on history, Karo spirit mediums, and the politics of representation.

Mick Taussig took a professorship at Columbia in 1987, leaving Mary with the challenges of writing her dissertation in his absence. Sherry Ortner, now department chair, stepped up to give Mary her engaged mentorship in the wake of Mick's departure. It also happened that Nicholas Dirks joined Michigan's anthropology department in 1987, and with Sherry founded the doctoral program in anthropology and history in 1988. Although Mary must have felt Mick's departure, Sherry and Nick's interest in history supplied an intellectual atmosphere and conversation in which Mary could continue to thrive.

Mary's breakout article, "Severing the Bonds of Love: A Case Study in Soul Loss," is a brilliant, piercing analysis of Karo Batak ceremonial curing practices.[14] Overlooked by most of us, it showcases Mary's deft handling of discursive fragments and contradictions so as to challenge analytic presumptions about cultural coherence and therapeutic efficacy, while also conveying something of the richness, humor, and open-endedness of curing rites "in the face of human suffering, fragmented lives, and unattainable ideals."[15] This is a memorable article, especially as it foreshadows Mary's theoretical orientations and her writerly craft.[16] It is her first publication, and the first in which she quotes a Karo curer describing the position of local spirit mediums as *"hanging without a rope, set down without a resting place"* (italics in the original).[17]

---

[10] See: George E. Marcus and Michael M. J. Fischer, *Anthropology as Cultural Critique: An Experimental Moment in the Human Sciences* (Chicago: University of Chicago Press, 1986); and James Clifford and George E. Marcus, eds., *Writing Culture: The Poetics and Politics of Ethnography* (Berkeley: University of California Press, 1986).

[11] Mary also spent time in 1986–87 studying and translating Batak bark manuscripts (for divination and ritual) collected by Harley Harris Bartlett during trips to northern Sumatra in 1918 and 1927, subsequently housed in the University of Michigan Herbarium.

[12] Marshall Sahlins had delivered a standing-room-only lecture at the University of Michigan in late 1981 or early 1982 that presented the core of his *Historical Metaphors and Mythical Realities: Structure in the Early History of the Sandwich Islands Kingdom* (Ann Arbor: University of Michigan Press, 1981) and what would be his *Islands of History* (Chicago: University of Chicago Press, 1985). Mary was there, but I recall she was not particularly drawn to the sort of historical analysis that Sahlins had outlined. ("Structure with dates," she once quipped.) I believe she much preferred the sorts of historical analyses coming from Subaltern Studies, or implicit in the work of her mentor, Mick Taussig.

[13] Benedict Anderson, *Imagined Communities: Reflections on the Origin and Spread of Nationalism* (London: Verso, 1983).

[14] Mary Margaret Steedly, "Severing the Bonds of Love: A Case Study in Soul Loss," *Social Science and Medicine* 27, 8 (1988).

[15] Steedly, "Severing the Bonds of Love," 844.

[16] "Severing the Bonds of Love" takes theoretical inspiration, in part, from ideas found in Frederic Jameson's *The Political Unconscious: Narrative as a Socially Symbolic Act* (Ithaca: Cornell University Press, 1982).

[17] Steedly, "Severing the Bonds of Love," 853.

Fragments of this essay would find their way into her first book and be put to powerful use in that extensive, beautifully crafted work.[18]

Mary joined Princeton's Institute for Advanced Study (IAS) in August 1988 as a research assistant for Clifford Geertz.[19] One thinks an assistantship with Geertz must have been a key opportunity or episode in "the making of an Indonesianist." From what I recollect of the time and what I can piece together from Mary's writings, however, I wonder if it wasn't Joan Scott, rather than Geertz, who had the more decisive impact on Mary's intellectual sensibilities during her year at IAS, and how she would bring them to bear on her ethnographic writing about the Karo. Most cultural anthropologists who studied anthropology and worked in Indonesia through the 1970s and '80s are in (some degree of) intellectual debt to Geertz. This is true of Mary (and of me, as well). But Scott's "Gender: A Useful Category of Historical Analysis"[20] and her debate with historian Linda Gordon about agency, power, and experience, published in 1990 in an exchange of book reviews and responses,[21] for me linger as spirit familiars in *Hanging without a Rope*.

While at IAS, Mary completed her dissertation and drafted what I believe would become her job talk to the Department of Anthropology at Harvard in 1990, "The Importance of Proper Names: Language and 'National' Identity in Colonial Karoland."[22] *Hanging without a Rope* came out in 1993, and like many who have written for this special issue, I took tremendous interest and inspiration from Chapter 6, "Someone Else Speaking."[23] The book would go on to win the Victor Turner Prize for Ethnographic Writing in 1994, an award shared with Lila Abu-Lughod's *Writing Women's Worlds*.[24] That prize assured Mary recognition as a rising star in anthropology. The year 1994 also saw Mary begin a new round of fieldwork in Karoland that would culminate in *Rifle Reports*.[25] I believe it is *Rifle Reports* that will endure as her most influential work in Indonesian studies, focused as it is on Indonesia's struggle for independence, and with its emphases on gender, memory, and the experience of hardship and struggle in northern Sumatra. But *Hanging without a Rope* holds a special place for me as the work in which her sensibilities—honed through years of scholarly labor; expanded through her acquaintance with Karo friends, intimates, and strangers; and driven, above all, by intense curiosity and nimble intellect—were put on such brilliant, extensive, original, and moving display. For me, it will always be a touchstone for any ethnographic work on the "outskirts" of Indonesia.

---

[18] Mary Margaret Steedly, *Hanging without a Rope: Narrative Experience in Colonial and Postcolonial Karoland* (Princeton: Princeton University Press, 1993); see chapter 2, "The Karo Social World."

[19] This was on Sherry Ortner's recommendation to Geertz, or so I recall being told.

[20] Joan Wallach Scott, "Gender: A Useful Category of Historical Analysis," *The American Historical Review* 91, 5 (1986).

[21] For Scott's debate with Gordon, see *Signs* 15, 4 (Summer 1990): 848–60.

[22] Revised, expanded, and published six years later in *American Ethnologist* 23, 3 (1996): 447–75.

[23] I put it to immediate use: I was teaching a lecture course at Harvard called "Life Stories: Culture, History, and Personal Experience," and for the 1994 session we read "Someone Else Speaking," and heard Mary guest lecture on her work.

[24] Lila Abu-Lughod, *Writing Women's Worlds* (Berkeley: University of California Press, 1993).

[25] Mary Margaret Steedly, *Rifle Reports: A Story of Indonesian Independence* (Berkeley: University of California Press, 2013).

• • •

I don't recall Mary and I ever exchanging manuscripts, or any bits and pieces of our writing about Indonesia, before the work made it into publication. It wasn't something we did. Our professional "conversations" and "work" together as Indonesianists and anthropologists were overshadowed by other enthusiasms that we shared—movies, Tarheel basketball, food, gossip about this or that. Indonesia was an animating and companionable force, or so I think, for several of her other friendships … not the only one, of course, but Indonesia counted as *the* place, or one of *the* places, where she and some Indonesianist friends discovered enduring bonds with one another. We never formally collaborated at Harvard save for a professional panel or two, and thoughts to co-teach a course in historical anthropology we would call "After the Indies" vanished when I decided to leave Harvard for the University of Oregon in 1996.

Mary's passing means I'm no longer able to share with her my memories of her becoming an anthropologist and Indonesianist, or to ask her, "Do you remember it this way?" If she were around to answer that question, I imagine she might reply, "Well, I remember having fun." Mary wrote to please, impress, and persuade others, to be sure. But she also wrote to please and amuse herself. Her wit and droll bemusement are signature features of her ethnographic storytelling, no less than her ear for (and rueful observations about) fragments of the strange, the ironic, the fleeting, or the supernatural in stagings of Karo and Indonesian sociopolitical worlds.

Ephemerality, Mary says in *Hanging without a Rope*, has to do with being excluded from narratives made durable through retellings and storytellers' ability to capture listeners' attention afresh.[26] Those colleagues and students who remember her in these pages, who have put her at the center of their thoughts and their own ethnographic work, have found ways to live with her still. With this special issue, they have written a moving and lasting epitaph for a wonderful ethnographer, storyteller, theorist, and Indonesianist.

---

[26] Steedly, *Hanging without a Rope*, 28–31.

MARY MARGARET STEEDLY: SELECTED PUBLICATIONS

The Editors

"Author's Response: Mary Margaret Steedly," in "Reviewed Work(s): *Rifle Reports: A Story of Indonesian Independence*, by Mary Margaret Steedly," *Sojourn* 30, 3 (November 2015): 869–76.

Rifle Reports: A Story of Indonesian Independence (Berkeley: University of California Press, 2013).

"Transparency and Apparition: Media Ghosts of Post-New Order Indonesia," in *Images That Move*, ed. Patricia Spyer and Mary Margaret Steedly (Sante Fe: School for Advanced Research Press, 2013), 257–94.

Patricia Spyer and Mary Margaret Steedly, eds., *Images That Move* (Sante Fe: School for Advanced Research Press, 2013).

"Modernity and the Memory Artist," *Comparative Studies in Society and History* 42, 4 (October 2000): 811–46.

"Surrogates, Slips, and Incidental Intrusions: The Tale of Raja Bakaléwat's Dog," *Anthropology and Humanism* 24, 2 (1999): 109–16.

"The State of Culture Theory in the Anthropology of Southeast Asia," *Annual Review of Anthropology* 28 (1999): 431–54.

"The Importance of Proper Names: Language and 'National' Identity in Colonial Karoland," *American Ethnologist* 23, 3 (1996): 447–75.

"What Is Culture? Does It Matter?" in *Field Work: Sites in Literary and Cultural Studies*, ed. Marjorie Garber, Paul B. Franklin, and Rebecca L. Walkowitz (New York: Routledge, 1996), 18–25.

Hanging without a Rope: Narrative Experience in Colonial and Postcolonial Karoland (Princeton: Princeton University Press, 1993).

"Severing the Bonds of Love: A Case Study in Soul Loss," *Social Science and Medicine* 27, 8 (1988): 841–56.

"The Evidence of Things Not Seen: Faith and Tradition in a Lumbee Healing Practice" (master's thesis, Curriculum in Folklore, University of North Carolina—Chapel Hill, 1979).

Jemma Purdey, Antje Missbach, and Dave McRae. *Indonesia: State & Society in Transition*. Boulder and London: Lynne Rienner, 2020. 261+ pp.

Robert W. Hefner

How are we to understand Indonesia today? Is it best viewed as the rare exception among Muslim-majority countries in having successfully transitioned to electoral democracy? Or is it more truthfully characterized as a fatally flawed oligarchic democracy plagued by money-politics and populist majoritarianism? More than twenty years after Indonesia's return to electoral democracy, questions like these continue to challenge Indonesianists. And it is against this background that Jemma Purdey, Antje Missbach, and Dave McRae offer a timely and intellectually bracing "survey of contemporary Indonesian politics, society, and culture, and its relations with the outside world" (2).

The authors bring varied skills to their task of making sense of Indonesia today. McRae is a senior lecturer at the Asia Institute at the University of Melbourne and author of one of the most important studies of communal violence in the early post-Suharto period, in the Poso region of Sulawesi.[1] Missbach is a lecturer in the school of social science at Monash University and the author of several important studies of migration, border regimes, and refugees in Indonesia and the Asia-Pacific.[2] Listed as lead author in this book, Jemma Purdey also teaches at Monash and has authored works on everything from Herb Feith and Australian-Indonesian relations to anti-Chinese prejudice in Indonesia; her *Anti-Chinese Violence in Indonesia* is a classic among studies of racialized violence in the late New Order period.[3]

With their high-octane credentials as Indonesianists, the authors divide their book into nine chapters, with the aim of "bringing together in one volume aspects of Indonesia's history, politics, international affairs, economics, and society to provide an overall picture of this complex nation" (vii). Chapter 1 opens with the question as to why a country as large, economically powerful, and strategic as Indonesia is "rarely included in lists of emerging powers" (1). The authors review Freedom House scores on the relative decline in the quality of democracy in Indonesia, and assess Gini coefficients to conclude that "inequality has increased steadily" (4). But their general analysis is balanced, noting that "Indonesia's performance in the political and economic spheres has been typical of nations of similar standing" (4).

Robert W. Hefner is professor of anthropology and global studies at the Pardee School of Global Affairs at Boston University.

[1] Dave McRae, *A Few Poorly Organised Men: Interreligious Violence in Poso, Indonesia* (Leiden: Brill, 2013).

[2] See, for example: Antje Missbach, *Troubled Transit: Asylum Seekers Stuck in Indonesia* (Singapore: ISEAS—Yusof Ishak Institute, 2015); and Antje Missbach and Wayne Palmer, "Indonesia: A Country Grappling with Migrant Protection at Home and Abroad," *Migration Information Source* (The Online Journal), September 19, 2018.

[3] Jemma Purdey, *Anti-Chinese Violence in Indonesia, 1996–1999* (Singapore: NUS Publishing, 2006).

Chapter 2 provides an overview of preindependence Indonesia, from the rise of Srivijaya and Mataram to the coming of Islam and Dutch colonialism. The chapter's historical current slows down and broadens as the authors turn to the late-colonial period and the birth of nationalism. They conclude with a tightly woven account of the war for independence, the ascent of Sukarno, and the challenge of national unity within a now mobilized society. Equally well-written, Chapter 3, "The Slide into Authoritarianism," reviews the rise of parliamentary democracy in the 1950s, the turn to Guided Democracy, the advance of the Indonesian Communist Party (Partai Komunis Indonesia, PKI), and the background and aftermath of the 1965 attempted coup, the Thirtieth of September Movement. The chapter then traces the deepening authoritarianism of Suharto's New Order, and ends with a short, two-page description of the fall of the New Order. The brevity of this last section may surprise some readers, but events surrounding Suharto's resignation were amply covered in Purdey's 2006 book. The chapter's conclusion highlights a theme at the core of the remainder of the book: "Although Suharto and a few others had handed over their power, there was little change in who held power, and, in the absence of a cohesive opposition movment … the new Habibie government carried over much from the previous regime" (59).

Chapter 4, "Political Reforms after 1998," opens with a discussion of regime continuities and reforms under the Habibie transition. "Habibie revoked several of the most visible pillars of authoritarianism" (63), especially with regard to elections, decentralization, and civil-military relations. The chapter ends with an incisive analysis of the communal and separatist violence that marked the early years of the Reform era. Chapter 5, "The Structures of Democratic-Era Politics," deepens this latter theme, exploring the background and consequences of decentralization, electoral reform, and money politics. This chapter also offers the book's most extended discussion of political Islam. Resonating with the analyses of Vedi Hadiz, and drawing on survey research by Marcus Mietzner and Diego Fassati, among others, the authors point out that some 46 percent of the Muslim public supports "seven elements of political Islam" (97), with even higher percentages supporting stern penalties for such hot-button items as blasphemy.

The book's narrative shifts in Chapter 6 from politics to health, education, and employment. The range of materials reviewed is impressive and well synthesized, touching on everything from demography and education (including a short discussion of Islamic schools) to poverty and unemployment. Chapter 7 extends the societal gaze to "Civil Society and Human Rights." The authors describe the repeated setbacks to efforts to achieve truth and reconciliation with regards to the killings of 1965–66 (in the aftermath of the Thirtieth of September Movement), and show the limits of state policy in Papua, Aceh, and East Timor. This chapter also has the book's most extended discussion of discrimination and violence against women, LGBTQ communities, religious minorities, and the disabled. Despite the pathbreaking reforms of the early *Reformsi* period, the authors soundly conclude that "the enforcement of human rights legislation remains problematic," owing largely to the continuing influence of "conservative forces within and outside government" (165).

Chapter 8, "Media and Popular Culture," provides the book's most extended cultural turn, situating media trends within a brilliantly analyzed structural context. The authors note that Indonesian media today are dominated by a small number of conglomerates, all linking news to e-commerce, gaming, and event management (168). They also show that the conservative turn among the Muslim public has impacted everything from soap-opera programming and film content to social media and censorship. Demonstrating again their eye for oft-overlooked details, they also cite studies showing that "Indonesian users spend an average of 3.5 hours a day on their internet or mobile device, 2.9 of those hours on social media" (185).

The book's final chapter examines Indonesia in world affairs. It outlines the impact of electoral pressures on Indonesian foreign policy, and, in a series of thoughtfully written chapter sections, highlights Indonesia's changing relationship with the United States, China, ASEAN, and the Muslim world. Returning to the question with which they opened their book, the authors observe that "Indonesia has yet to play a role in international politics commensurate with its vast territory, strategic position, and large population" (222). Nonetheless, there is a widespread expectation in the international community that Indonesia's influence will continue to grow.

In a book as far-ranging as this one, it is inevitable that some issues—to my eye, for example, Muslim mass organizations, and especially Muslim women's organizations—get short shrift. Regardless, few topical stones are otherwise left unturned in this engagingly well-written and expansive book. In both its range and policy balance, this book is a significant achievement, and deserves to be read by all with an interest in Indonesian politics and society today.

Nobuto Yamamoto. *Censorship in Colonial Indonesia, 1901–1942*. Leiden: Brill, 2019. 294 pp.

John Ingleson

The much-cherished *rust en orde* (tranquillity and order) of late colonial Indonesia was underpinned by a highly developed surveillance state. From the 1910s the state became worried about nationalist, labor, and religious movements stirring up the simple natives and threatening *rust en orde*. It responded by restructuring the police force, strengthening the mobile police brigade, and creating a political intelligence service that reported directly to the attorney general in Batavia. The political intelligence service recruited hundreds of informers in major towns and cities who needed to report in regularly to justify their retainers. They produced detailed, if not always accurate, reports on meetings of Indonesian organizations, and provided documents from closed meetings of nationalist parties and labor unions as well as a steady stream of rumors. Indonesian political and labor union leaders were well aware that informers attended their public meetings—they were hard to miss, as they usually sat in the front row and were often the target of humorous asides from speakers. These political and union leaders also knew that informers had infiltrated their organizations and regularly warned of the need to exercise caution and expel suspects. The federation of Sumatra plantation companies had its own intelligence service from the mid-1920s, employing informers on estates who produced regular reports, often of an alarming nature, about workers' activities. Dutch managers of plantations, sugar mills, and major companies were constantly alert for signs of political infection among their Indonesian workforces. At the first sign of worker protest, such managers telephoned the local resident or police superintendent, who would invariably send a posse of the police armed mobile brigade (Korps Brigade Mobil, Brimob) for a show of force or to make arrests. The territorial army was the ultimate weapon of state control. Strategically located throughout the colony, it was used during the large railway strike in 1923 to patrol railway stations and workers' neighborhoods as well as to evict strikers from their company-provided homes. After the failed PKI (Partai Komunis Indonesia, Communist Party of Indonesia) rebellion of late 1926 and early 1927, the army was instructed to revise its plans for direct intervention in labor or political unrest. Surveillance and police and military intervention was backed by draconian laws that saw thousands of political and union activists jailed in the 1920s and 1930s, and under the constant threat of being exiled to Boven Digul, the prison camp in West Irian specially created for political prisoners after the failed communist rebellion.

Censorship in Colonial Indonesia is an extended analysis of another important instrument of the surveillance state in its constant effort to control not only what people did but also what they said and wrote. In discussing the state's surveillance of newspapers and periodicals in the last three decades of colonial rule, Yamamoto focuses on the two major instruments of censorship: the *persdelict* (press offences) and

---

John Ingleson is emeritus professor of history, School of Humanities and Languages, University of New South Wales.

persbreidel (press restriction) laws. Modeled on the British India Press Act of 1910, the prohibition on publishing *persdelict* articles was added to the colony's Penal Code in 1914. The types of articles considered *persdelict* were wide-ranging and their definitions broad, thereby making prosecutions difficult to defend. The writer of an article that expressed or instigated feelings of hostility, hatred, or contempt against the Netherlands or the Indies government could be jailed for up to seven years. Complemented by the even more encompassing "hate sowing" articles of 1923 and 1926,[1] the *persdelict* law was a powerful weapon that the colonial state could and did wield against those it considered a threat to *rust en orde*.

There is an excellent chapter on the ways in which the colonial authorities applied the *persdelict* and the ways in which journalists responded. Yamamoto argues that there were three major responses: defiance, compliance, and diversion and defamation. The first response is illustrated with a detailed account of the trial of union and communist party leader Semaun in 1919; the second with an analysis of the writings of the Batavia journalist Parada Harahap; and the third with an examination of the Chinese-Malay press. Yamamoto shows how prosecutions such as that of Semaun enabled Indonesians to take advantage of court proceedings because Indonesian newspapers were free to report on those proceedings. Yamamoto's discussion of Semaun's trial includes an extensive translation of his defense speech. This English-language translation is a welcome addition to the well-known defense speeches of Hatta and Sukarno.

The *persbreidel* was an added instrument of control introduced in September 1931, under which the governor-general could ban the publication of any newspaper or periodical that he believed threatened public order. Whereas the *perdelict* required prosecution in an open court, thereby providing a platform for the accused, the *persbreidel* enabled the governor-general to make unilateral administrative decisions, thereby denying the accused a public soapbox. It was one more instrument in the armory of the colonial state that sidelined the open courts. Introducing *persbreidel* was also one of the last actions of Governor-General De Graeff, but, as Yamamoto notes, he had made the decision to introduce it a year earlier, on August 17, 1930, after considering conflicting advice. Was it a coincidence that this was just one day before the opening of the trial of PNI (Partai Nasional Indonesia, Indonesian National Party) leaders Sukarno, Gatot Mangkupradja, Maskun, and Supriadinata in the Banding District Court? Probably not. De Graeff had chosen not to use his *exorbitant rechten* (extraordinary powers) to exile the PNI leaders outside Java rather than put them on trial. For some time, he had doubted his decision to authorize their arrest and worried that his decision to prosecute them in an open court would provide them with an opportunity to deliver a strong attack on colonial rule. He knew that this would be reported by every major Indonesian newspaper. His fears were justified. Sukarno's lengthy and powerful defense—*Indonesia Accuses*—was published widely.[2]

---

[1] The "hate sowing" articles were added to the penal code in 1923 and 1926. Article "161 bis" banned strikes or advocacy of strikes, with a penalty of up to five years' imprisonment; articles "153 bis" and "153 ter" penalized speeches, writings, or pictures that threatened tranquility and order, either directly or indirectly, or by veiled suggestion or by implication, with a penalty of up to six years' imprisonment.

[2] See, for example, Soekarno, *Indonesia Accuses! Soekarno's Defence Oration in the Political Trial of 1930* (Oxford: Oxford University Press, 1975).

Yamamoto has made good use of the diverse files in the Ministry of Colonies in order to provide a comprehensive discussion of the debates on how to control the written word both within the colonial government and between Batavia and The Hague. He rightly argues that the censorship laws directed at newspapers and other publications were the "invisible hand" that journalists and editors had to respect, and could never know for sure the laws' limits of tolerance. That, of course, made them all the more likely to engage in self-censorship in order to protect themselves.

Yamamoto shows that these censorship laws were used to combat different problems during different political circumstances. The *persdelict* was aimed at Indonesian nationalists and radical Muslims in the 1910s and 1920s, when the European community in Indonesia was shaken by the rise of nationalism and, more particularly, the growth of the Indonesian communist party. The *persbreidel* had a broader remit. It was used against the Dutch language press as well as the Indonesian press during the difficult Depression years (1930–36), but from the mid 1930s was directed largely against the Chinese language press. Having tamed the nationalist movement, by the mid 1930s the colonial government's major security concern was the expansion of Japanese economic and political influence in Southeast Asia. The *persbreidel* enabled the Dutch to clamp down on anything that might antagonize Japan after the intensification of Japan's military incursion into China, in particular anti-Japanese sentiment among Chinese in Indonesia, both native-born (*peranakan*) and those born in China (*totok*). A nervous colonial government used the *persbreidel* to punish Chinese-owned newspapers that published anti-Japan articles by attacking the newspapers' economic base.

Yamamoto has made good use of Dutch and Japanese sources on the colonial government's engagement with Japanese consuls in Surabaya, Semarang, and Batavia regarding anti-Japan articles in the Chinese-Indonesian-owned press. There is also a discussion of Japanese economic and cultural penetration in Southeast Asia in general and Indonesia in particular in the 1930s, including its involvement in financing newspapers, influencing journalists, and spreading pan-Asian ideas. Japanese penetration of the printing business was seen by colonial authorities as a major threat. It responded with the Printing Regulation in April 1935 that allowed it to control printing companies, including compelling divestment. The *persdelict*, the *persbreidel*, and the printing regulations, in conjunction with the "hate-sowing" articles, the governor-generals *exorbitant rechten*, and the ever-present threat of being sent to Boven Digul was a formidable repressive arsenal.

In order to implement the *persdelict* and *persbreidel* laws the colonial state was dependent on translated summaries of articles from the Indonesian and Chinese language press that were produced and published each week by Balai Pustaka (Bureau for Popular Culture). The summary, called IPO (Overzicht van de Inlandsche Pers), was widely circulated among Dutch officials in the colony, as well as among officials at the Ministry of Colonies. For many it was required reading. Yamamoto discusses the people that produced these reports, the newspapers and periodicals they regularly surveyed, their changing categorization over time, and the criteria for article selection. The IPO weekly surveys were not always accurate summaries, as historians who have compared them to the original articles can attest, and they provided only a partial and often biased view of the contents of newspapers and periodicals. It is therefore not surprising that Dutch officials who relied on IPO summaries to understand what "the natives" were thinking, because they did not or could not read the press themselves, failed to see, let alone understand, the deeper forces at work in Indonesian society.

Censorship in Colonial Indonesia includes a large number of tables and appendices meticulously constructed from scattered files in the Ministry of Colonies and contemporary publications that will be a valuable resource for future historians. These include detailed lists of *persdelict* cases, the names of journalists charged, and the eighty-seven actions taken under *persbreidel* between 1931 and 1942. There are also tables containing lists of Chinese- and Indonesian-language newspapers and periodicals published during the last decades of colonial rule, the ownership of printing businesses, and the number of newspapers delivered by mail broken down by major cities. *Censorship in Colonial Indonesia* provides an important contribution to our understanding of the surveillance state of late colonial Indonesia.

Tim Lindsey and Simon Butt. *Indonesian Law*. Oxford: Oxford University Press, 2018. 576 pp.

Jeremy J. Kingsley

A book titled *Indonesian Law* at first glance suggests an ambitious undertaking. Even though I know Tim Lindsey and Simon Butt are both knowledgeable and leading scholars of Indonesian law, at the outset I was concerned about overreach in terms of the book's scope. With these words of caution, it is good to be proven wrong. As soon as one opens this book it is hard not to recognize the breadth, and importantly, depth, of this publication.

Essentially, it is a remarkably fine reference book outlining Indonesian law. It provides a framework for understanding and learning the broad parameters of Indonesia's substantive law and legal institutions. This will be a useful resource for students, legal professionals, and scholars of Indonesian law, and acts as a sound starting point to contextualize the Indonesian legal system and its impact on Indonesian society.

Having studied Indonesian law and its legal culture for over a decade, I still found this text to be enlightening and a rich source of information on the Indonesian legal system. It provides a clear outline of substantive Indonesian law and the many issues affecting this civil law jurisdiction. The text is organized into five parts (Legal System, Land Law, Criminal Law, Commercial Law, and Private Law) and then expounded through twenty-two chapters that give life to these larger legal categories. This structure helps to arrange the substantive discussions in a coherent and straightforward manner.

The one criticism of this book that I would make is that it could be studied in a decontextualized manner. Indonesian legal culture(s) and socio-political affairs are largely skirted over. The editorial reason for this choice is understandable in that it is a reference book of the Indonesian legal system and laws. However, some readers may inadvertently overlook context and, if not careful, read their own assumptions about law and its practice into the Indonesian situation. It would, therefore, be useful to read this book alongside other leading texts on Indonesia law.[1]

Even with this criticism, it is hard not to recognize that this book makes an outstanding contribution to our understanding of Indonesia's legal system. It is a must-read reference for all scholars and professionals working in or learning about Indonesia … not just legal scholars. *Indonesian Law* contextualizes the functioning and activity of law and statecraft in a comprehensive and authoritative manner.

The utility of this book comes from allowing scholars, students, and professionals to understand the structures and boundaries and, therefore, limitations of Indonesian

---

Jeremy J. Kingsley is a senior lecturer and director of Swinburne Law School's Indonesia Law, Governance, and Culture Program.

[1] For instance, see: Tim Lindsey, ed., *Indonesia: Law and Society* (Annandale: Federation Press, 2008); and Sebastiaan Pompe, *The Indonesian Supreme Court: A Study of Institutional Collapse* (Ithaca: Southeast Asia Program Publications, 2005).

law. It is not about reading this cover-to-cover. Rather, this reference book has particular sections that no doubt are vital to scholars engaged in different aspects of Indonesian political, media commentary, digital affairs, economic studies, and cultural life. It is easy to look at the deficiencies of Indonesian law and therefore avoid treating it with due respect and recognition. This book should put to rest such negative considerations and, consequently, provides a useful resource to assist people to engage with and recognize the importance and limitations of the Indonesian legal system and its relevance to their interests.

Susie Protschky. *Photographic Subjects: Monarchy and Visual Culture in Colonial Indonesia.* Manchester: Manchester University Press, 2019. 244 pp.

Arnout van der Meer

Most scholars of the late-colonial era in Indonesian history will be familiar with the peculiar omnipresence of the Dutch Queen Wilhelmina (r. 1898–1948). Her name is forever associated with the announcement of the "Ethical Policy" in 1901, with spectacles organized in her honor, such as Batavia's (Jakarta) extravagant annual fair, and with political resistance, like Suwardi Suryaningrat's attempt to raise money with his infamous anticolonial pamphlet, "If I were a Dutchman," to petition Wilhelmina for greater political liberties. Even in the vernacular press, especially publications sponsored by the colonial authorities, her image was a common feature. For instance, the initial four issues of *Bintang Hindia* (Star of the Indies)—a richly illustrated biweekly periodical for the educated elite among the colonized—featured Wilhelmina, her husband, and her mother on its covers.[1] Through these photographs of the queen, the readers of *Bintang Hindia* were introduced to *their* monarch in far-flung Europe. It is therefore surprising that the representation of Wilhelmina, and the Dutch monarchy in general, in colonial Indonesia has received scant attention from scholars. Susie Protschky's latest monograph, *Photographic Subjects: Monarchy and Visual Culture in Colonial Indonesia,* addresses this lacuna.

Photographic Subjects departs from the deceptively straightforward premise that while Queen Wilhelmina was physically absent, she was very much pictorially present in colonial Indonesia. None of the Dutch monarchs ever toured their empire in Asia prior to independence movements there. Among the reasons offered for ruling from afar were practical concerns over temporarily abandoning governance of The Netherlands as well as anxieties over the possible health and safety hazards that accompanied travel in the tropics. Protschky adds to this list an intriguing reason for the queen's absence, namely, the fear that her physical appearance would underwhelm the colonized who were used to pomp and splendor from their own rulers. It was in this particular context that the symbolic representation of a distant sublime sovereign, enabled by the advent of mass photography that coincided with Wilhelmina's reign, proved expedient. Photographs, according to Protschky, "emerged as the most ubiquitous proxy for [Wilhelmina's] absent self in the colonies" (12). In her book, Protschky explores the many ways in which people in the Indies—colonizer and colonized—engaged with these images of the queen, which at times helped to construct a transnational sense of community and belonging as well as reinforcing social and colonial hierarchies. In other words, photographs were an important vector in the communication of power—not only its exercise, but also its contestation. It is through a study of these photographs of the Dutch monarch that Protschky, in a highly original manner, adds to our understanding of the entanglement of Indonesian and Dutch histories.

Arnout van der Meer is assistant professor of history, Colby College.

[1] *Bintang Hindia,* nos. 1–4 (1902).

As the title of Protschky's book indicates, this is not a study about Queen Wilhelmina's, or the Dutch monarchy's, personal connection and interaction with colonial Indonesia. The focus instead is on how subjects—Dutch and Indonesian—in the colonial world engaged with the monarchy through photographs. Protschky therefore examines not only photos of the royals themselves, but primarily pictures of their subjects during royal celebrations in the colony. Through a careful examination of these fascinating images she illustrates how "positions of agency and subjecthood were articulated on these occasions through photography" (208). Protschky's arguments are supported by no fewer than sixty-three (!) photographs, which all hail from archival collections in The Netherlands. Two kinds of photographic sources stand out in this study. First, Protschky draws extensively on family albums, a source rarely used by scholars thus far. Second, she examines photographs preserved in the Royal Collections in The Hague that originally were gifts from Javanese Principalities to the Dutch monarchy as a means to assess how Javanese royalty positioned themselves in relationship to the Dutch monarch. Taken together, this is an invaluable contribution to the existing scholarship, consisting of the work of Karen Strassler and Protschky's earlier work on photography, modernity, and identity in colonial Indonesia.[2]

Protschky convincingly demonstrates how pictographic representations of the Dutch Queen compensated for her absence by communicating power and instilling a sense of association within a larger transnational community. This happened in both familiar representations (e.g., state portraits at colonial offices and residences) and in more surprising ways, foremost through an annual royal spectacle. Throughout the Dutch empire, the week commemorating the Queen's birthday (August 31) and inauguration (September 6) was filled with public celebrations and ceremonies. Protschky uses photos from these festivals to show how portraits of Wilhelmina were treated almost as effigies in public rituals. Queen's Day (*Koninginnedag*) was celebrated wherever there was a colonial representation in the Indies—in major cities and provincial towns, from Java to the other islands of the archipelago. Most of these celebrations included singing the Dutch national anthem (the *Wilhelmus*, named after Wilhelmina's ancestor), both in Dutch and Malay; a procession that often included a photograph or bust of the Queen; public games; performances; and fairs. These were carefully orchestrated spectacles, bringing to mind Clifford Geertz's concept of the "Theatre State," which reinforced local colonial authority by association with a distant monarch.[3] In addition, by looking at family albums, Protschky shows how it was the "synchronicity with events in the Netherlands" that reinforced a sense of belonging among Dutch citizens in the colony (66).

The concept of modernity is a recurring theme throughout the book, which is a continuation of an interest Protschky pursued before as editor of two excellent volumes.[4] In this study, she explores the visual representation of the alleged enlightened Wilhelmine rule in colonial Indonesia. Protschky argues that although

---

[2] See: Karen Strassler, *Refracted Visions: Popular Photography and National Modernity in Java* (Durham: Duke University Press, 2010); and Susie Protschky, ed., *Photography, Modernity and the Governed in Late-Colonial Indonesia* (Amsterdam: Amsterdam University Press, 2015).

[3] Clifford Geertz, *Negara: The Theatre State in Nineteenth-Century Bali* (Princeton: Princeton University Press, 1980), 13.

[4] See: Protschky, *Photography, Modernity and the Governed*; and Susie Protschky and Tom van den Berge, ed., *Modern Times in Southeast Asia, 1920s–1970s* (Leiden: Brill, 2018).

Wilhelmina did little to deserve the lasting association with progressive colonial policies, besides announcing the Ethical Policy in 1901 (the Dutch civilizing mission), this connection was visually promoted through pictures. Photographers especially captured electric illuminations at royal celebrations in the colony, which presented modern conveniences (such as electricity and infrastructural improvements) as the beneficial successes of Dutch rule. In this manner, Protschky argues, a new "visual language for celebrating monarchy and empire" (88) emerged that emphasized Dutch modernity and contrasted it deliberately with indigenous tradition (e.g., ceremonies for Javanese rulers were only pictured in the daylight). The conflation of electricity, modernity, and royal celebrations was a form of soft power that legitimized colonial authority to the indigenous observer. In this light, it is a pity that Protschky did not engage more with photographs of Batavia's Pasar Gambir (the annual fair held in Wilhelmina's honor), which was undoubtedly the largest electrically illuminated spectacle in colonial Indonesia.[5]

One of the most intriguing parts of Protschky's book explores the ways in which Javanese royals defined and negotiated their relationship with the Dutch monarchy through gifts of photographs to the queen. Of the four Javanese principalities, only the head of the house of Mangkunegaran visited Wilhelmina in The Netherlands; the other three Javanese rulers refused to submit themselves as vassals in person. Instead, they engaged in what Protschky aptly describes as "snapshot diplomacy" by using photographs to delineate their own sovereign position vis-à-vis the queen (120). Javanese royals exerted agency over the composition of these images, in which Protschky both identifies acts of accommodation as well as resistance. For instance, in certain photographs the Javanese rulers wore the honors bestowed by the House of Orange in combination with Western and Javanese dress, signaling both their modernity and rootedness in Javanese tradition as sources of their status and position. Remarkably, they also had themselves depicted with only a single spouse, whereas they were all polygamous, as a clear concession to Dutch taste and conventions. But there were clear signs of contestation, too, such as the averted gaze of Susuhunan Pakubuwono X of Surakarta in a photograph from 1937, indicating his refusal to submit to the viewer, Queen Wilhelmina. Sultan Hamengkubuwono VII of Yogyakarta went even further in not including any pictures of himself in his offerings to the queen, a symbolic manner of presenting himself as her equal.

At some points in the book the reader is left wanting more. This is in part the result of Protschky's methodology, which privileges the photographic record in studying the past. But one of the aims of the book, to establish the appeal of the Dutch monarchy among the colonized, is not entirely resolved. Whereas previous studies suggested that the Dutch monarchy primarily appealed to Western-educated elites, Protschky's study suggests a much broader segment of the Indonesian people was reached by the orchestrated royal spectacles.[6] However, the photographic record does not reveal to what extent the Dutch monarch was taken to heart. To establish this, if at all possible, a more complete examination of the Indonesian perspective is required, for instance, through a study of the vernacular press, literature, and biographies. This could shed

---

[5] Y. N. Lukito, "Colonial Exhibition and a Laboratory of Modernity: Hybrid Architecture at Batavia's Pasar Gambir," *Indonesia* 100: 77–103.

[6] G. Oostindië, *De Parels en de Kroon: Het Koningshuis en de Koloniën* (Amsterdam: De Bezige Bij, 2006).

light on how Indonesians experienced and interpreted the celebration of Queen's Day and what it meant to them. Did the queen make a lasting or a fleeting impression? And finally, the reader is left to wonder whether the archives could help in uncovering Wilhelmina's own opinion about and influence on the way she was projected overseas. Did she have a hand in how she was portrayed? How did she make sense of the complex relationship between monarchy and empire?

In sum, *Photographic Subjects* is an original contribution that is extensively researched and thoroughly engaged with the broader literature and theoretical frameworks on empire, photography, modernity, and late colonial Indonesia. For both scholars and students interested in these fields, this is an indispensable read.

Jan Mrázek. *Wayang & Its Doubles: Javanese Puppet Theatre, Television and the Internet.* Singapore: National University of Singapore Press, 2019. 349+ pp.

Miguel Escobar Varela

This book chronicles the history of *wayang kulit*'s presentation in television and the internet through situated testimonies from a variety of people: artists, producers, sponsors, spectators, and academics. These voices are interspersed with the author's own experiences watching *wayang*—live, on television, and online—over two and a half decades. The book shows how *wayang* is transformed when it is presented via television, but also indirectly changed by it, as the aesthetics and aspirations of *wayang* respond to television's allure and broad cultural influence. Television, too, is transformed in this process—*wayang* serves as a litmus test of what television can or should accomplish, and what its roles should be in Indonesia. Thus, Mrázek characterizes the ways in which *wayang* and television transform each other as a "marriage full of conflicts," where each consort is transformed by its interaction with the other. These interactions are not limited to specific events, but also encompass the ways in which key *wayang* and television stakeholders imagine and misunderstand each other. *Wayang* and television, in Mrázek's analysis, are "haunted" by each other's specters. This haunting is further complicated by the arrival of the internet, which in many ways realizes the dreams that early television broadcasts could not achieve (for example, the direct transmission of all-night performances), but also continues old problems, such as the clashes over intellectual property ownership between different "cultures of copyright." Thus, the internet and television are characterized as *wayang*'s doubles: spectral, half-imagined representations of itself. As the author notes, this is "a story midway between reality and imagination" (204).

To tackle this story in all its complexity, the book invites us to see television as *wayang*'s conflictive consort, and also as its double. Mrázek's analysis artfully combines these two metaphors to bring humor, nuance, and depth to a variety of points he makes throughout the book. These shifting metaphors emphasize plurality (there are many *wayangs* and many televisions), and long histories (while *wayang* is transformed by television, *wayang*'s contemporary features also owe much to processes that started much earlier). These evocative metaphors are put into conversation with the ideas of Martin Heidegger, Maurice Merleau-Ponty, Jaques Derrida, Paul Virilio, Max Weber, and James Siegel, among others. In the author's words, "I do not apply their theories or methods, but rather shamelessly localize their thoughts and gather them into one coffee shop, so to speak, with those of Javanese practitioners, *wayang* audiences, and theorists, as well as with my observations and reflections" (7). The coffee-shop-as-method gives the book its distinctive tone and structure. Take, for example, the way in which Heidegger's ideas are brought to bear upon the discussion: "Sitting with *Mbah* Martin in the coffee shop, we may playfully substitute *wayang* and television—each is a mode of revealing, of truth, but each involves a different way of being in the world" (14).

Miguel Escobar Varela, an assistant professor of theater studies at the National University of Singapore and an academic advisor at the NUS Libraries, is also a web developer, translator, and theater researcher; and he is active with the websites Contemporary Wayang Archive and Digital Humanities Singapore.

Heidegger is referred to as "*Mbah*," the honorific used for respected elders. This device is not just for levity's sake: it nuances and re-contextualizes Heidegger's points, and brings them into conversation with other ideas, in an attempt to move "from gossip to philosophical and mystical ruminations, from personal anecdotes to historical reflections, from observations on what is happening at this particular *wayang* event to what someone read in a book about *wayang*, with reflections and observations interwoven somewhat like the voices in the many-layered texture of Javanese gamelan music" (9).

Thus, wit and wisdom are brought together to highlight culturally specific problems and conditions. Readers familiar with Mrázek's previous work might recognize a familiar style in these playful passages. In his introduction to *Puppet Theater in Contemporary Indonesia*, Mrázek imagines each contributing author as a *wayang* puppet.[1] In his *Phenomenology of a Puppet Theatre*, the footnotes often add humor and incisiveness to the writing.[2]

In this book's coffee shop, we don't only hear from the theorists of media and society, but also from producers, aficionados, puppeteers, and sponsors who live and work in Java. This multiplicity of voices presents a nuanced and complex picture that doesn't fit easy narratives. As Mrázek notes, this is "a story of unfinished projects and broken or forgotten promises; a fragmented, non-Aristotelian story without a beginning, 'logical' causal progress, and a conclusion" (204). See, for instance, how clashes between producers and *dhalangs* are portrayed. In Chapter 1, Mrázek recounts an encounter with Handoko—who was at the time of the interview the president of the Indosiar television station—in a fancy, glass-paneled office in Jakarta. Handoko is adamant on presenting "authentic *wayang*," but when Mrázek questions him on his programming choices, the executive replies in English: "what we need is ratings" (36). As the author notes, the executive's perspective negates the complexity of *wayang* as an event, and of the people who watch it for a wide variety of reasons. This is not a politically neutral perspective, and Mrázek systematically unpacks the history and politics that make such a statement even possible. He then shows how views such as those espoused by this producer lead to misunderstandings with the *dhalangs*. But it would be disingenuous to extrapolate from this exchange, and derive a general rule on the behavior of producers. Later in the book, Mrázek introduces another producer, Habib Bari, who was the president of TVRI Yogyakarta in the 1970s. In an interview in Yogyakarta, Habib Bari offers a radically different perspective, which is highly critical of producers from Jakarta:

> The *dhalang*, of course, has a high status. Javanese people say he has received a boon from the gods [*wahyuning dewa*]. Now, if the young kids [i.e., television producers] who have no manners/etiquette [*kirang tatakramanipun*], [tell the *dhalang*] directly, just like that, "This must be done like this, this must be like that [*ini nanti harus begini, harus begitu*]"—well, [the *dhalang*] does not want [to follow]. I have never had any problems, but as I said, the manner of approaching [the puppeteer] must use Javanese culture [*cara anggenipun nyelaki*

---

[1] Jan Mrázek, ed., *Puppet Theater in Contemporary Indonesia: New Approaches to Performance Events* (Ann Arbor: University of Michigan Press, 2002).

[2] Jan Mrázek, *Phenomenology of a Puppet Theatre: Contemplations on the Art of Javanese Wayang Kulit* (Leiden: KITLV Press, 2005).

kedah ngangge budhaya Jawi]. The kids today are always in a hurry. [...] In the world of *wayang*, I consider the *dhalang* omnipotent [*mahakuwaos*]" (210; brackets in original).

Passages such as this will be a delight for readers conversant in Javanese and Indonesian. But Mrázek's attentive glossing also indicates the code switching and cultural sensitivity of his interlocutor. More importantly, the quote above attests to the nuanced, complex tapestry of voices invoked in the book, which counter simplistic narratives of the media and its politics in Indonesia. The combination of voices in the book also includes different authorial voices: Mrázek and his doubles. The first few chapters are written from the era of Indosiar (1990s) in present tense (a move justified through Merleau-Ponty's dictum to "write in the present"), and the rest of the chapters explore what happened after and before this period. Chapter 1 considers how *wayang* is imagined for television (and how it, in turn, reimagines television). To be suitable for television, *wayang* is made brighter, easier to understand, shorter, and sexier. These changes cannot be entirely credited to television's influence, as they are the result of a longer, anxious engagement with modernity. Mrázek charts how *wayang* has become more realistic over an extended period of time, and how recently this "realism" is equated with life as seen on television, which often means the "realism" of cartoons on TV. Thus, Mrázek warns us that interaction with modernity is something to be taken with a pinch of salt: "If *wayang* is able to see and show its televisation and modernization as a comedy, as a masquerade, it means that we have to be careful how to interpret any move towards television" (77). Chapter 2 pays special attention to the conflicts between producers and *dhalangs*, although this is a preoccupation that permeates the rest of the book (as seen from the excerpts above). Chapter 3 considers the phenomenology of watching *wayang*, live or on television, both through the author's perspective and through those of his interlocutors. Chapter 4 looks at experiments before the "Indosiar era," where this was the dominant station presenting *wayang*, and up to the watershed moment of 2005 when local TV networks flourished and internet transmissions began in earnest.

Chapter 5 considers what happened later. Although this final chapter deals with more recent materials, one of its goals is to show that the interaction of *wayang* and the internet is not entirely new, but that it continues previous fantasies and fears, and provides new possibilities for old sources of nostalgia, creative dreams, and power struggles. A particularly memorable segment is the analysis of live YouTube comments (288–304), where a Javanese diasporic community rejoices in their communal watching, sharing in excitement and nostalgia in real-time. A disclaimer: my own work on *wayang* and the internet is positively reviewed in this chapter. Thus, readers of this review might wish to take my enthusiastic response to Mrázek's book with a dose of suspicion. But perhaps another way to take my disclaimer is to see my review as personal and situated, and thus as an appropriate response to Mrázek's book. His is a playful, personal, and deeply researched account of a complex topic. *Wayang and Its Doubles* invites us to play by its own rules, but in exchange it offers a relentless attention to nuance and contradiction rarely seen in academic works. The book is an enjoyable and thorough account of slippery ontologies, where media exists as fantasy and reality, and where voices overlap, contradict each other and themselves, and change over time.

This brings me to a last point of how I see the potential contribution of this book. It is doubtless a major addition to the scholarship of very recent Javanese *wayang kulit* developments—a field with a wide range of debates and findings that had so far been mainly developed through dissertations, book chapters, and articles (for example, by Matthew Cohen, Marianna Lis, Kathryn Emerson, Kristina Tannenbaum, and Sadiah Boonstra). The book will also be interesting to scholars of the performing arts elsewhere in Indonesia and throughout Southeast Asia. But it should also attract the attention of researchers interested in how mass media and digital platforms are changing culture. Many books—indeed, large academic fields—are concerned with what happens to culture as the world moves online. The task is onerous and it is easy to offer simplistic explanations. But this book offers a lesson on the importance of sustained ethnographic and historical attention. It is a careful reading of conversations and their gaps, of artifacts and their doubles, where history is circular and discontinuous rather than linear and evolutionary, and where contradictions and mismatched expectations are presented in their full spectrum. It is all too easy to offer simplistic narratives of television and the internet: what they bring and what they take away. Much harder and rarer is a book that takes these contradictions at face value and digs into longer genealogies to present "a story in which people's actions, ideals, and dreams, formed in the encounters between people and technology and between different media and their cultures, are only imperfectly controlled by consciousness" (204). Mrázek's work is an invaluable source of methodological inspiration on how to portray the textured, messy clashes of tradition, mass media, and the internet in Indonesia and beyond.

David Bourchier. *Illiberal Democracy in Indonesia: The Ideology of the Family State.* Abingdon: Routledge, 2015. 318 pp.

Jeffrey A. Winters

There is a game of social-cultural generalizations that pretty much everyone engages in. New Yorkers are said to be brash. American midwesterners are nicer folk. Italians indulge their passions. Brits are reserved. In the Indonesian context, the Javanese hate confrontation and won't reveal what they're really thinking. Bataks are loud and relish a debate. The Madurese and Ambonese are warmhearted, but quick-tempered.

Heads nod as various complementary or insulting things get said about broad populations, even though we know these are stereotypes that fall apart quickly at the level of actual individuals in each group.

As David Bourchier reminds us in this excellent book, it is a very different phenomenon when powerful actors and states engage in a parallel game of generalizations about the character of their people. The difference lies in the motives. Contending factions of elites are interested in stable control and smooth domination, and they work hard to manufacture political-cultural interpretations that advance these goals.

Indonesia's leaders aggressively promote the view that from the basic family unit, up through villages and neighborhoods, and on to the national level, Indonesians are a people who value harmony above all else and prefer to operate by consensus rather than by voting. Political opposition, dissenting parties, and general disagreement are labeled as un-Indonesian, and a commitment to individual political and human rights is derided as a Western import. Authentic Indonesian politics is portrayed as a harmonious family with the nation's leaders playing the role of benevolent parents. Permanently positioned below are the citizens as obedient and grateful children. Bourchier notes that this vision has been variously called organicist, corporatist, and integralist. It is also a key ideological ingredient of authoritarianism—and especially of fascism.

Defining Indonesia's social and political identity has been a contested terrain for over a century. Bourchier's analysis of illiberal democracy in Indonesia arrived just as new clashes have erupted over what constitutes a true, authentic, and good Indonesian. The work provides a sophisticated framework for understanding the origins and trajectory of these debates and it deserves to be read widely.

What is at stake in these clashes is not actually discovering who Indonesians are at their core. That is a pointless exercise even for societies that have a great deal of homogeneity. For diverse countries like Indonesia, it is an absolute impossibility. Indonesians are many things depending on their class, gender, and ethnicity, and the socio-cultural trajectories of their lives. Some are empowered while many are

---

Jeffrey A. Winters is professor of political science and director of the Equality Development and Globalization Studies Program, Northwestern University.

marginalized. The country's history makes clear that Indonesians resist when they can and go along when they must. Their identities are dynamic and may overlap in various ways with the constructed political culture. But there is also an endless array of subcultures and countercultures.

Elite investments in national-identity narratives serve two important purposes. Vertically, and most obviously, the goal is to render the population docile by glorifying a natural and harmonious hierarchy that delegitimizes dissent and resistance. But there is a horizontal purpose as well. Those in power must fend off competing elite factions (ambitious aunts and uncles, perhaps?) who think *they* should be in charge of Indonesia's big, happy family. Along the way, the masses below endure heavy doses of *gotong-royong* (mutual assistance) indoctrination, while at the elite level Indonesians conduct an intricate dance of *bagi-bagi* (sharing of the spoils) to keep the extended family leadership from stirring up mischief.

The broad outlines of the story in *Illiberal Democracy* are familiar. But what Bourchier accomplishes in this book is to provide the most comprehensive examination to date of how this conservative ideology of domination arose and evolved in Indonesia. He also adds an important historical dimension rooted in European political philosophy. Prior to Bourchier, the most important and pathbreaking scholarship on the topic was by David Reeve and Marsillam Simanjuntak.[1] It is useful to think of Bourchier's contribution as positioned between these two major analysts. Reeve's arguments, which largely accepted the view that Indonesians have an authoritarian-subservient bent, were so broad that important distinctions could not be made between the philosophies of such major figures as Supomo, Sukarno, and Hatta. Simanjuntak's study of Indonesia's integralistic state was both an exploration and a rejection of the authoritarian-subservient interpretation of Indonesian culture and political philosophy. But it was excessively narrow in that it centered mostly on the debates and outcomes around developing Indonesia's 1945 constitution.

Bourchier deepens the analysis by providing much more nuance about the range of political philosophies Indonesian leaders have formulated and pushed. Equally important, he delivers a devastating blow to the "foreign import" critiques of democracy and liberalism by showing that the conservative and authoritarian ideologies favored by Indonesia's leaders are Western and Japanese imports as well. The real debate is not whether major ideological streams in Indonesia are strongly influenced by outside thinkers. Rather, it is *which* of the outside influences supposedly resonated best with what is authentically Indonesian. That answer depends on what aspects of Indonesian society and culture elites set out to discover, emphasize, and amplify. Anyone determined to see competition, oppositions, dissent, individualism, conflict, resistance, and robust debate across Indonesian history and society will find

---

[1] See: David Reeve, *Golkar of Indonesia: An Alternative to the Party System* (Oxford: Oxford University Press, 1985); David Reeve, "The Corporatist State: The Case of Golkar," in *State and Civil Society in Indonesia*, ed. Arief Budiman (Melbourne: Monash University, 1990), 151–76; Marsillam Simanjuntak, "Unsur Hegelian dalam Pandangan Negara Integralistik" (Master of Law thesis, University of Indonesia, 1989); and Marsillam Simanjuntak, *Pandangan Negara Integralistik: Sumber, Unsur, dan Riwayatnya dalam Persiapan UUD 1945* (Jakarta: Pustaka Utama Grafiti, 1994). Also noteworthy for its emphasis on the gendered character of the family state ideology is Julia I. Suryakusuma's seminal MA thesis, *State Ibuism: The Social Construction of Womanhood in New Order Indonesia* (Institute of Social Studies, The Hague, 1988), published under the same title in 2011 (Depok: Komunitas Bambu).

abundant evidence of all of these views and behaviors. But that is not what most Indonesian elites were looking for and not what they found. Bourchier does a masterful job of explaining why and how this was so.

The book spans ten chapters relying primarily on a rich collection of secondary sources. One of the study's signal contributions is to assemble elements from various works on Indonesia into a coherent thesis about the origins and development of the country's dominant political philosophies. The early chapters emphasize external influences on the Indonesians who formulated the nation's political identity. Especially with regard to the role of reactionary Dutch and German philosophers and teachers, Bourchier traces how the first Indonesian students in Europe, especially those studying law at Leiden University, were introduced to organicist ideas that they would bring back to the colony and apply to the project of national identity formation and national liberation. He amplifies these influences in a chapter focusing on the Japanese, whose conservative nationalist ideas were also strongly shaped by the same European thinkers. The key vector for Japan's imprint on Indonesia's anti-democratic and anti-liberal forces was through military officers rather than lawyers.

The next two chapters focus on the emergence of Indonesia's nationalist movement, the important debates surrounding the 1945 constitution, and the Sukarno years. Thanks to the revolution against the Dutch and the mobilization from below that this necessarily entailed, organicism and "family state" notions suffered setbacks as more progressive elements of Indonesia's elite became important players in framing who Indonesians were and what their struggles meant. Conservatives, to their great dismay, themselves became targets of sustained criticism from democratic progressives. This resulted in integralistic figures like Supomo losing key battles over the character of the constitution. From 1945 until at least 1956, proponents of reactionary "family state" concepts found themselves on the defensive. Bourchier nicely explains how President Sukarno and General Nasution, both eager to grab more power, moved in tandem to the right to advance a corporatist "guided democracy" version of Indonesian politics that set the stage for Suharto's full embrace of the family state ideology.

The next four chapters focus on Suharto's New Order, his use of organicist ideologies to disempower both the masses and elite political opponents, and the force-feeding of a version of *Pancasila* that emphasized hierarchy, obedience, and the illegitimacy of opposition and dissent. The last of these New Order chapters traces how the family state ideology was attacked and undermined by prominent Indonesian intellectuals during the final decade of the dictatorship. While these sections provide a useful overview for those studying Indonesia for the first time, they are mostly a review for seasoned Indonesianists.

The book's epilogue focuses on the revival of *Pancasila*, which has unfolded along two tracks. The first, most notably pushed by Prabowo's Gerindra Party, is in the classic reactionary tradition dating back to the ideas of the Leiden lawyers and those of their Japanese-influenced comrades in the armed forces. The second, coming from Megawati's Democratic Party of Struggle (Indonesian Partai Demokrasi Indonesia-Perjuangan, PDIP), is more surprising, but also perhaps problematic for Bourchier's argument. This strain is a desperate effort to invoke Indonesia's dominant national ideology to counter the intolerance of political Islam.

It is the ideology of Islamic religionism, which has been sweeping across Indonesia's political landscape since the early 1990s, that Bourchier does not engage. It represents the ambitions and interests of a faction of the country's elites who want to replace more secular forms of domination with a theocracy they control. It would be valuable to explore where this competing conservative ideology overlaps with the organicists, and where it departs. Rather than drawing on *adat* legal notions, for instance, the Islamists have long opposed these traditions as incompatible with Islam's core religious precepts. The family state is certainly patriarchal, but not quite in the same way that Islam is.

What is so important about all of this, and why it is regrettable that Bourchier did not give us a chapter that addresses religious ideological currents in Indonesia, is that those struggling hardest to contain political Islam and counter its domination of women or its intolerance of religious minorities or other marginalized groups are, ironically, turning to *Pancasila* and all that is "authentically" and "indigenously" Indonesian to subvert the Arab and Middle Eastern thrust of the new religious orthodoxy. The counter-narrative to a caliphate in Indonesia is not focused on democracy, human rights, or secular empowerment from below. Instead, it invokes some of the same reactionary themes Bourchier traces and dissects so brilliantly throughout his book. In the end, Indonesians are mostly locked within conservative ideological clashes exclusively on the right. But now the battle is between antidemocratic philosophical influences imported from Europe and Japan versus those imported from the Middle East. It is left to the reader to sort out how the ideational foundations Bourchier lays so well are playing out in the face of the ideologies of political Islam.

www.ingramcontent.com/pod-product-compliance
Lightning Source LLC
Chambersburg PA
CBHW080636230426
43663CB00016B/2895